Sister,
I FEEL YA

Sister, I FEEL YA

A WAKE-UP CALL
FOR WOMEN OF FAITH

KIM DAFFERNER

ENCOURAGE
PUBLISHING

Printed in the United States of America

For worldwide distribution.

Library of Congress Control Number 2022943067

Cataloguing data:

Dafferner, Kim

Sister, I Feel Ya: A Wake-up Call to Women of Faith

1. Persuasion (Psychology) 2. Marriage (Sociology) 3. The Christian Life (Religion—Philosophy) 4. Christian Living—Love and marriage 5. Christian Living—Spiritual growth 6. Christian Living—Personal growth 7. Christian Living—Women's issues

Dewey Decimal Classification: 248: Christian experience, practice, life

Cover and interior design by Jonathan Lewis

Cover photo by Meredith Smith

Edited by Leslie Turner

Scripture quotations marked (ESV) are taken from the Holy Bible, English Standard Version, ESV® Text Edition® (2016), copyright © 2001 by Crossway Bibles, a publishing ministry of Good News Publishers. All rights reserved.

Scripture quotations marked (MSG) are taken from The Message. Copyright © by Eugene H. Peterson 1993, 2002, 2018. Used by permission of NavPress. All rights reserved. Represented by Tyndale House Publishers Inc.

Scripture quotations marked (NLT) are taken from Holy Bible, New Living Translation, copyright © 1996, 2004, 2015 by Tyndale House Foundation. Used by permission of Tyndale House Publishers, Inc., Carol Stream, Illinois 60188. All rights reserved

ISBN 978-1-9601660-0-5 (paperback)

ISBN 978-1-7343231-8-4 (hardback)

Published by:

Encourage Publishing, New Albany, Indiana

www.encouragepublishing.com

For Henry.

Contents

Foreword

KRISTIN FUNSTON

Christian speaker and author of "More for Mom: Living Your Whole and Holy Life"

I **JUST WANT THESE** women to know what the Bible actually says!" she exclaimed sitting back in the kitchen chair, bright red ponytail bouncing back and forth with a head shake.

Yes and amen, sister.

We were sitting at our pastor's kitchen table, nose deep in our Bibles and several biblical commentaries. We spent lots of hours sitting together at that table over the next weeks, prepping to teach the book of Esther at an upcoming women's retreat. This was the first time I met Kim Dafferner, and she was everything I had heard she was before that first meeting... bubbly, outgoing, and on-fire for the Lord.

I remember this particular statement because it had been something burdening my own heart for a while... and still does; wondering how many women knew what the Bible truly says, not just what *other people* say it says. Because—at the risk of sounding ridiculously redundant—it is the Bible that says what the Bible *actually says*.

What the Bible says—the stories, lessons, and Truth found in it—is not always what you'll find in the latest Christian podcast, latest devotional book, or even the latest and greatest online sermon. I have to admit, as a Christian author and speaker, I take the risk of losing readers and listeners by pointing them back to the Bible, instead of my own books and speaking events or even this book you're reading right now.

While the Christian self-help row at the local bookstore or your local women's ministry events are so, so good, they are not *the* Truth we need. They can enhance it, help make it more clear, and help motivate us to read it, but they aren't the *actual* Bible.

This is what Christian women need to know: it is the Bible alone that gives us direction and perspective for a life that will sustain us through to the end. It is the Bible, coupled with our messy lives, that reveals our need for and redemption through Jesus.

The Bible reveals Jesus.

The problem is fewer and fewer of us know what the Bible actually says. Every day, fewer and fewer people in our country know what it means to truly live a life that not just *believes* in, but *follows* Christ.

Here is the good news: we were never meant to turn against the current of culture and follow Jesus alone. God Himself, as a triune God, is the very definition of community, and He not only allows, but invites us into community with other believers.

This is why we crave community — it's built into us. We crave to be seen and heard and known by others. It is why we crave to hear the words "me too."

We know we need these words. We know we need community and trusted friends and family to do life alongside and for someone to simply 'get it.' But I think we forget it's not just *any* type of encouragement we need... we need *biblical* encouragement — other people to, at times, speak hard Truths to us when we've slightly gone off course, pointing us back in the Way.

We are so used to hearing, "you do you" or "I'll support you in whatever makes you happy" or "live your own truth," or some other nice-sounding, but not-truly-kind, sentiment of support. This is when it's critical to hear Biblical truth. We may not *want* it, but we *need* it. This is why the book you're holding is such a strong breath of fresh air.

In the short time I've known her, this is how it is with Kim — you go deep, you go biblical, and you do it together. Not one to beat around the bush, she jumps directly to scripture in her conversations, yet not neglecting the realities of our day-to-day lives.

Since that first day studying the book of Esther together, I've seen Kim's burden to share the gospel. She's the person who isn't scared to ask a stranger if they know Jesus or not and the person who always has an answer to those who wonder about the Hope inside of her. And maybe even more importantly, she's also the one to continue diving into Scripture daily to learn more from and about her God.

Every interaction with Kim — either in person or through the pages of this book — are met with gregarious energy. She meets you with open, interested eyes, and a thousand watt smile. Even reading her words, you can almost hear her feisty and sweet southern drawl, and see her head nod in agreement as she empathizes and encourages us to look to Jesus for guidance, comfort, and to act out in His Truth.

I'm grateful for this book. These hard truths are some we might only hear from a trusted friend. I pray you'll let Kim's bold sense of humor, her wisdom, and genuine empathy be that friend for you today.

Sister, you're about to be blessed...

Kristin Funston

Sister, let's get started.

LET'S START WITH a pointed question. Really think about what I am about to ask you because this entire book rests on how you answer.

Are you a sleeping Christian? I'll word it differently. In your walk with Jesus, have you become a little too chill? Have you become too comfortable with the busyness and rhythms of life to really grasp Jesus in all of it? Do you go through the motions with little regard of being made for more? In other words, has your faith become complacent?

Being complacent is not a good thing if you're a Christian. You see, complacency and Christianity are an oxymoron. They don't make sense when used together. You can't claim Jesus and park it in the complacency garage. If you're a Christian, Jesus should set your soul on fire. I get that there is a level of routine in any relationship, but, y'all, this is Jesus—your Creator. He dwells in you. You should feel different. You should be compelled to want to be different. Some of you may know that already. You know you're bored in the worst of ways. You know you should be moved but you just don't desire that right now. You may be angry. You may be sad. You may have doubts. All of this is okay. But you have to be honest with yourself. Because here's the scary thing. You may be complacent in your faith and have no idea. You may be slipping farther and farther away from him because, well, you are asleep. Sister, I am praying over you right now as I write. I am praying that something I say will penetrate your soul and you will wake up.

If this is you, you are not alone. There is no condemnation in my words. Only urgency. The truth is, so many of us who know Jesus are angry, sad, complacent—and fast asleep. Snoozing through church. Snoozing through community. Snoozing at home. Snoozing while our children are being indoctrinated by the world. Snoozing through marriage. Snoozing

1

through life. We have to wake up! This book is about waking up, about losing the facade and returning to Jesus right where you are. Come with your questions. Come with your hurts. Come with your doubts. Come with your sin. Don't suppress it. Just come.

"But…" we keep saying.

"No, buts," God keeps reminding us.

No "buts," sister. There are no "buts" when God is speaking. My biggest prayer is that you close this book feeling encouraged. Relieved. Amped up. *Awake.* Full of grace. Hopeful. *More* in love with your life and with the people *in* your life. Most importantly, *more* in love with Jesus. I want you to feel a sense of revival in your soul knowing that your thoughts, your private laments, and your deepest struggles have no reason for shame. I want you to feel *more* empowered to take them to the one who died for you. In the midst of your failures, your struggles, your shortcomings, and your bondage, while you are sleeping, there is someone who loves you *more* than you will ever comprehend. There is nothing you can do or say or be that will shake the love of Jesus off you. He is all in. Put a ring on it. Matching tattoos–committed to you whether you feel it or not. It's a hard thing to grasp, I know, but that doesn't change the fact that it's yours for the taking.

My hope is that you will find the courage to admit you relate to your struggling sisters. Me. The one at church. The one at work. The one at the grocery store. Because they need you. I need you. And honestly, you need us too. Before I wrote this book, I fought the process. The growth. The exposure. All of it. The thought of putting myself out there for anyone to know the real me is frightening, and I certainly don't take criticism like a champ; I take it like a sissy. But if I can connect with you over all the things I've hidden over the years, all the things I have unsuccessfully tried to numb, I'm willing to completely expose myself, *because here's the deal: I need you to wake up.* I want you so badly to lean into Jesus, to come to really know him, and to let his words speak fire into your soul. I want you to *want* to be different *because* of him. Even in your sin. Even in your struggle. Listen, the struggle is the best part! That's where you see the God of the Bible show off his glory in you. That's where you see Jesus take your sin, your insecurities, and your fears and redeem them. Prepare to have your socks knocked off!

I know this sounds crazy, but I love you. Even if I haven't met you, I love you. And since we can't talk over coffee in some rustic coffee shop or have a glass of wine by an outdoor fire pit or eat endless baskets of chips and salsa, know that I am on my knees praying for Jesus to woo you back to him. And one day, one beautiful day, all these struggles will be a thing of the past. And we will have heaven. *And then, the party is on!*

But until that day comes, we have to do the work—the hard, messy, uncomfortable work. But you aren't alone. We have each other! Together, we can cut through the distractions. We can work through the complacency. We can revive the dead parts of our soul in church, in our community, with our Bibles, and in prayer. But you have to be awake to do it!

1

Sister, what are you hiding?

Truth and courage aren't always
comfortable, but they're never weakness.
Brené Brown

WHEN I HAD my first son, I gained forty pounds. I lost most of the weight eventually, but I wore yoga pants for the longest time. He also didn't sleep through the night for a while, so I was a hot mess. I remember walking into my first mom's group at a local church when he was a few weeks old. I was so excited to bond with other moms over this whole newborn thing. I was so ready to have people normalize my feelings and tell me all the things that I didn't know about parenting. I had been pretty isolated, so this group was a step in the right direction. Christian fellowship and camaraderie were finally in my sight. I had high expectations to say the least. I was a little insecure when I arrived at my little mom's group, so I sat back and listened as these five or so women talked about life.

Y'all, I couldn't bring myself to go back. This experience was mind-blowing. I felt like a little girl who used all her hard-earned piggy bank money to buy an ice cream cone, only to drop it on the hot pavement. One beautiful new mom mentioned she wore her pre-pregnancy jeans home from the hospital, instantly making me feel like a beached whale in my stretchy yoga pants. While I silently struggled with bleeding nipples and sleep deprivation, a more experienced mom's advice filled me with dread. She told us she nursed her three babies all for two years and never drank caffeine or ate processed foods just in case God blessed her with a fourth. I was pounding coffee and eating fast food the second they cut my son's umbilical cord. Then there was the sweet little mama who said her amazing husband delivered their baby, and she didn't need an epidural because of her home water birth. I pretty much asked for an epidural on the way to the hospital, and did I mention that every time I coughed, the stitches in my lower region popped? That and the fact that I pooped on the delivery table.

I wasn't jealous of these ladies, except for the skinny jeans girl. Dang. I was too crushed to be jealous. I felt like I had been sucker punched. There I was, feeling fat, still bleeding, and new to the fold. Literally, my only accomplishment at this point was keeping my baby alive. That and I had finally managed to go number two. But in all seriousness, I needed these women to come alongside me and tell me it would get better. They had no idea I had wrapped so much need into that first visit. They had two hours of my time to share their "first" stories and ease my insecure heart. I needed their listening ears, their encouragement, and their wisdom. I needed to be seen and heard with compassion. Instead, as the moms continued to glow in their accomplishments, I reflected on the ways I didn't measure up. I was fat. My pre-pregnancy pants were a thing of the past. I was sleep deprived and mean to my husband. But most of all I was scared. Scared that I would accidentally hurt my baby. Scared I would be a bad mom. Scared of SIDS. Scared my husband would never look at me with lover's eyes again after seeing the whole birthing process. *Will we ever have sex again? What if my kid doesn't love Jesus?*

Here's the thing. You may be very impressive. I was impressed by the fact that someone could nurse three babies for two years and still manage to have perky boobs. I was equally impressed that someone's husband wasn't horrified by the things coming out of her body during childbirth. I would be lying if I told you I wasn't impressed with the girl who was able to get back in her jeans twenty-four hours after giving birth. Seriously, high-five, awesome, impressive stuff. But do you know what I wasn't? I wasn't seen. I wasn't empowered. I didn't leave feeling closer to Jesus. I don't think anyone intentionally alienated me. Perhaps they were just like me. Maybe some were compensating for their own insecurities and their own need to be accepted. Can you imagine what would have happened had we all been able to set aside our insecurities, knock down our walls, and just be authentic with each other?

All that to say, my visit to the mom's group wasn't a complete bust. I did leave better, because that meeting was a turning point for me. After that meeting, I was determined to be the kind of woman who gets it. To be the friend who understands. At that moment I realized that I would be anything for God, even if it meant making a fool of myself. I still haven't mastered this, but God left a mark on me that day. He reminded me that he doesn't need us to be perfect. *He* is perfect. *He* is awesome. He wants to do awesome things in us and through us. He simply needs *us* to be obedient. That day, God called me to be relatable. Vulnerable. Real. Sisters, who is with me?

Here's the deal. Some starry-eyed intern at work may think you're the most brilliant woman on the planet because you're smart and juggle so many balls perfectly. Some young mom may look to you and think you have it all together with your Girl Scout preparedness and immaculate home. Some lady in your Bible study may be in awe of your perfect body. These people may be impressed by your product, the life you've created, but what about the process? What about your struggle? What about your journey? People aren't drawn to Jesus by our accomplishments. People are drawn to Jesus when they see him in our transformation. In our failure. In our pain. In our mess. And sometimes, yes, when we finally do get it together. The point is, people need to see *him*—not you and not me. And I'm convinced that sharing only the highlights of our lives to our accountability group does not reflect Jesus. Pretending we are something we're not in no way magnifies our savior. If this is your mask, I get it. I do it too, usually out of insecurity. Regardless of the "why" of your disguise, it still renders the same negative results. It alienates *you*, it alienates *others*—and it's exhausting. Sister, take your mask off.

> **People aren't drawn to Jesus by our accomplishments. People are drawn to Jesus when they see him in our transformation.**

I believe that most of our truth filters are set on autopilot. In order to prove my point, let's do a little exercise. Let's look back at our last week of social media posts or think back to last week at church or even with our friends. What did you share? Here's a more personal question. What *didn't* you share? Did you tell your friends at church that life is great when, in fact, you are dying inside? Did you share your heart with a close friend? Or did you talk about *anything else* in order to avoid the deep, dark stuff? Does anyone know that you are struggling to keep it together? Listen, if you only post your Sunday best on social media, if you pretend like your biggest problem is your grandmother's upcoming hip surgery when in fact you are in a dark place, hear this next part loud and clear. You are wearing a mask. Not that I'm asking you to pour your soul out on social media or overshare in Bible study. But what I am asking of you, pleading with you, is for you to be real with yourself. Be real with those closest to you. Quit the facade, feel what you need to feel, and be real with Jesus, above all. The truth is, we connect with people through our weaknesses. And, those weaknesses are the exact backdrop that magnifies Jesus.

Some time ago God put on my heart that he wanted me to be more vocal for him, write another book, post more on social media, spread my wings so to speak. Basically, he asked me to put myself out there for him. Around that same time, I began meeting with a woman who was struggling in her marriage. Full disclosure, my own marriage did not start off well. In fact, I spent the first seven years of my marriage contemplating divorce. I even prayed my husband would die a time or two (more on that later I promise). Gasp, I know. Stay with me here, because I promise you, if you have never felt this kind of pain in a relationship, someone you know and love has. My own marriage journey is precisely why God put this woman in my path. I could relate to her pain. I could share my struggle with her. Now, I'll share it with you.

My husband grew up with a family that didn't talk about their deep feelings much. His parents are wonderfully supportive and kind as all get-out, but talking about their everyday feelings just wasn't a thing for them. My family was just the opposite. My parents constantly told me I was beautiful and could do anything. We talked about every feeling at all times. My dad used to get me a flower every Easter Sunday that I proudly wore like a prize. Clad with my white hat, I was daddy's little princess. My mom was just as doting. Whenever we would get in a fight, she always, I mean always, wrote me a letter to apologize and clear the air.

When Andrew and I got married, listen, there was no flower. There was no sitting in anyone's lap being told how amazing I am. There was definitely no letter after a fight. Shoot, there was hardly pillow talk. For close to seven years I wanted out. I was miserable, and daddy's little princess deserved more. For years I would walk into church heavy-hearted. I wouldn't get close to anyone for fear they would find out about my secret. I hated my life because I lived it as if everything was perfect, knowing I had one foot out of the door. I felt like a failure and a fraud.

Here's my point. For close to seven years, I walked around secretly miserable. I lifted my hands in worship. I attended Bible studies, I was in weddings, I went to baby showers—all the while I was crumbling inside. While I posted on social media that I was living my best life with my best friend, while I had babies, what I wouldn't have given for someone to have read through me and said, "Kim, I see through the facade. It's time to take your mask off."

Every Sunday, every single Sunday since that season, I walk into church and wonder how many women are as miserable as I was. How many women feel like a fraud? How many women feel like their pain is too embarrassing to share? How many women want out? How many women are struggling with being a mom? How many couples are neck deep in credit card debt? How many are depressed, perhaps suicidal? How many women hate the way they look, or the life they have built? How many drown alone in a sea of other women? How many?

Andrew and I have come a long way—I now know he is a rock star and the perfect man for me, but our marriage is far from faultless. One thing I love about him is that he doesn't feel pressured to adapt to his environment. It doesn't matter if you are his college buddy or the pope; if he says a cuss word, he says a cuss word. If he wants a beer, he has a beer. He's consistent. I remember telling the Lord (first mistake—"telling" God anything) that there was no way I could share the gospel and pour into anyone if my own husband cussed and drank beer in front of them. "How on earth can I offer hope to women when my own husband cusses and drinks?" I complained.

You know what God told me? He reminded me that my husband's imperfections and struggles with sin are exactly why he *can* use me.

My own self-righteous attitude that my sins are somehow not as bad as my husband's sins is exactly why I *should* surround myself with other women. The faulty idea that I ought to be able to "control" my husband is exactly why I *should* speak life into marriages; my own shortcomings and imperfections are *why* he can use me. And guess what? Your weaknesses are why God can use you, because they make you relatable. Our struggles inspire hope. That in itself is ministry. That in itself is life-giving to others—and reason number 999 as to why we need to take our masks off.

Do you struggle to keep the perfect home, or maintain the perfect body? I don't know about you, but I relax a little when I walk into someone's house and see stains on couches or dog hair on the floor. I have a hard time relating to someone who is perfectly disciplined with macro counting. I want to know that this whole balance thing is a struggle for everyone. I believe it's this struggle that brings us together, that teaches us grace, and helps us point one another back to Jesus. In all honesty, I would have a hard time receiving advice from someone who doesn't admit that they have struggled, too. We have to do this life together, and the best way I know is to surround ourselves with honest sinners who do not want to stay complacent in their sin. When we are honest about *our* struggles, we can trust these very same people to point us back to Jesus. And when they struggle, they can call us and know we will get real, pray for them, and then point *them* back to Jesus. This is what Jesus had in mind when he modeled the importance of community. In fact, Hebrews 10 says:

> And let us consider how to stir up one another to love and good works, not neglecting to meet together, as is the habit of some, but encouraging one another.
>
> Hebrews 10:24-25 (ESV)

But I suck, you might be thinking. *You don't know my past. You don't know my track record.*

Let me tell you about this guy named Moses. He's kind of a big deal. *With God*, he led the Israelites out of slavery. *With God*, he parted the Red Sea. *With God*, he delivered the Ten Commandments. But before God called him to do great things, Moses was far from being the kind of person you would trust with such responsibility. Seriously, if you ever feel insecure or inadequate read about Moses in Exodus. He murdered someone because he couldn't control his righteous anger, and then he ran away and left his family behind. He also had a speech impediment, a flaw that is a massive struggle for anyone, much less a leader. But God delights in weaknesses. He delights in imperfections. And he delights in idiots like me and you—and Moses. If you don't remember the backstory that led to this unlikely hero, read Exodus 2–4. The truth is, God chooses whom he chooses, and he chose Moses, who wasn't particularly excited about it. Have you been there? When God told Moses he was the guy to free God's people, I hear my own shortcomings in Moses' response.

Moses: "But why me?"

Insert your own self-doubt here. "Why do you want *me* to lead other women? Why do you want *me* to be the one who takes a stand at work? Why do you want *me* to teach? Why do you want *me* to adopt?" What's your "why me" insecurity? Take a second to really think about it. What is God asking you to do? Now ask yourself why you think you can't do it.

God: "I'll be with you."

At first, it seemed ludicrous to me that God talked to Moses and promised his full support, yet Moses still doubted. If I were God I probably would have spit fire out of the burning bush and moved on. Yet we respond just like Moses, don't we? God may not talk to us through a burning bush, but he most certainly does speak to us through the Holy Spirit and through his Word. And guess what? When we question God, he doesn't spit fire on us, either. In fact, I think he welcomes our questions.

Moses: "Send somebody else."

I've often thought these very thoughts. "God, ask my sister. She's a pastor's wife. Or ask that girl who already has ten thousand followers on Instagram or that woman I work with. She's smarter. She's prettier. She is funnier. She can write better. I've always been awkward. I'm not articulate." Again, insert your own insecurity here.

I am God. I will bring you out from under the cruel hard labor of Egypt. I will rescue you from slavery. I will redeem you, intervening with great acts of judgment. I'll take you as my own people and I'll be God to you. You'll know that I am God, your God who brings you out from under the cruel hard labor of Egypt. I'll bring you into the

*land that I promised to give Abraham, Isaac, and Jacob and give it
to you as your own country. I AM GOD.*

Exodus 6:6–8 (MSG)

Boom! He will bring us out of our bondage. *Boom!* He will call us
his own. *Boom!* The same God in the Bible, the God of all these great
men in Genesis—the God of Moses—*that* God will be God to *us. Boom-
chick-a-boom!* You can't tell, but my heart is pumping as I type this. If
I were saying this to your face I'd be shouting! Forget your inadequacy,
it doesn't matter! He chose *you!* Big nose? No problem. Chubby? Who
cares? College dropout? Forget about it. Poor? Not an issue. Sketchy past?
No biggie. Why? Because none of this matters. He wants to be awesome
in you and, more importantly, through you.

Moses: "I stutter." (Oh my goodness, here he goes again.)

Moses: "I stutter." (And again.)

I realize that most of us don't stutter. But we all have some issue holding us back. Some insecurity. Some reason why we don't come forward.
We all have something we're hiding. Some reason we choose to only
share the good. It's why we smile and keep it light in small group but are
secretly dying inside. We all have some reason why we don't live out our
purpose. We think we are ugly. We have a secret. We hate our marriage.
We are living in debt. Sister, what's in the way?

In Genesis 3, Adam and Eve felt shame after sinning so they covered
themselves with fig leaves. This was the ramification of their sin and their
shame. That was never God's intended design. Adam and Eve were never
meant to live naked and unashamed. *We* are not meant to live naked
and unashamed. Obviously, that doesn't mean we need to walk around
in the nude. But our souls? Our souls are meant to be in the buff. Our
deep-rooted guts are meant to be bare. We aren't supposed to feel shame
in that. Do you hear what I'm saying? That sin. That flaw. That insecurity.
That secret. Bare it to Jesus. Then, bare it to a human being. Bare it on
a blog. Bare it to your Sunday school class or to a counselor. It doesn't
matter. Just ditch the fig leaves and bare it.

So, here's my question to you. What shame are you covering with fig
leaves? What shortcoming? What pain? What insecurities? What part
of your soul is clothed? Whatever it is, expose it. Take the fig leaves off.
Remove the "I'm naturally skinny" mask and confess that you may have

an eating disorder. There are women dying to connect with you over this. There's a Savior eager to bring them to you. Quit the "my kids are my greatest joy" comments and admit that some days you wish they were in daycare. There are other moms out there who need to have their feelings normalized. There are other moms who would love to talk about the fact that staying home with your kids is harder than going to work. How about exposing this over Chick-fil-A nuggets instead of pretending that you have the greatest life on the planet?

> **Share your shortcomings, pain, and insecurities.**
> **There are other moms who need to have**
> **their feelings normalized.**

Quit the "my marriage is so awesome" posts on social media when the truth is you are struggling. Instead, admit to a trusted friend that life without him sometimes seems easier. Or that he struggles with porn. Or that you have thoughts about a man you work with. Tell your best friend. Tell your Bible study leader. Tell someone. Let them walk through this with you. Then, when God redeems your situation, because I promise you he will, you can be relatable to someone else. You can use your sin, your addiction, your struggling marriage, your insecurities, and have a platform for Jesus. You can say those words I so badly needed to hear the day I went to that mom's group. You can be the vulnerable, courageous girl who rips her fig leaves off and utters those simple words we struggling women are dying to hear: "Sister, I feel ya."

He comes alongside us when we go through hard times, and before you know it, he brings us alongside someone else who is going through hard times so that we can be there for that person just as God was there for us.

2 Corinthians 1:4 (MSG)

2

Sister, who are you?

*The fear of not being enough and the fear
of being "too much" are exactly the same
fear. The fear of being you.*

Nayyirah Waheed

DID YOU EVER have one of those childhood dreams that was so cute but so ridiculous at the same time? You know, the ones where you want to be a princess or an astronaut or the first female president? Well, I have one. I have always, I mean always, wanted to be a CIA agent. I made the mistake of telling my brother one time, and he reminded me that I'm scared of the dark. He's actually right. The other day I turned off all the lights after everyone was asleep and I sprinted up the stairs like Usain Bolt because obviously Chucky was behind me. You laugh but I know you've done this. Maybe with the shower curtain? Before you sit down to "potty," you know you draw it open while you duck. Or how about always checking the back of the car before you get in it? (Okay, this may be a good idea.) Despite my fears and silly paranoias, I still somehow want to be in the CIA. Whenever I watch TV shows and movies, I don't want to be the damsel being rescued by some Gerard Butler type. Heck no. I want to point my gun with confidence and save the world. That confidence. That stoicism. I would love to possess those qualities. But I don't have them.

Truth is, I struggle with the fact that I'm none of those things. I'm actually the antithesis of all of them, and I've always known that. I remember doing this Halloween craft in kindergarten. We were supposed to cut out a witch and glue it to a piece of construction paper. Pretty simple and straightforward, right? Not for me. I was rocking my witch project only to look up and see that mine was different. Apparently, I glued her hair sticking straight up to the moon instead of falling gracefully on her shoulders like my classmates' witches. I know it's a silly thing to remember, but that's the first memory I have of being different. It's kind of sad, really. You don't realize you're different until you're around people outside your circle. At home my parents thought I was so cute. They would call me clever when I asked things like, "What if the whole world farted at once?" I remember my Sunday school teacher delighting in the fact that I asked a million questions. As a young kid, I was so confident. I felt normal. I felt like someone who blended in with everyone else. I thought I was vanilla, only I wasn't. I didn't realize I was different until I stepped into the real world and saw that I was some sort of cosmic rainbow flavor, that asking a million questions was not "normal"—it was annoying. Hearing the question "Do you ever stop talking?" haunts me. The phrase "You say the weirdest things" can still deflate my spirit.

Do you have a story like this? Do you possess some weird trait that's not "normal"? Do you have some odd behavior or way of thinking that you try to hide? The year was 1986 when I first realized I did. It was actually the beginning of events that had me feeling lonely most of my young life. And misunderstood. And begging God to wire me like everyone else—to "un-weird" me if you will. Oh, how this kind of prayer, this kind of thinking, has to break the Father's heart to hear. It's like telling an artist their art sucks. Can you imagine your child asking you to make them different? I wish I could go back and tell my younger self to take heart. I wish you would believe me when I tell you to be okay with how God created you. To actually thank him for the way he created you. Besides, "normal" doesn't exist. That put-together girl in Bible study? She's not normal. That mother-in-law of yours? Nope. That lady at work? She isn't normal, either. "Normal" is a facade. Sometimes it's a mask worn on purpose. Other times it's a conclusion you come to on your own. Either way, normal is not a thing. So do me a favor. Think about your own "weird." Think about your gifts. Think about the stories that have shaped you.

Think about what sets you apart from others. Now, ditch the facade and embrace the sparkle. God's children aren't made to be vanilla. We are made to be cosmic rainbow flavored. You aren't vanilla. Stop pretending to be.

You aren't vanilla. Stop pretending to be.

Maybe my story doesn't resonate at all. You may think you're normal and vanilla. You may even think I'm an absolute weirdo. Perhaps you killed it with crafts in elementary school. You may have felt loved and cherished in high school. Shoot, you may have dated the captain of the football team. You may have been in the best sorority and married some cute frat boy and moved to the suburbs. Your cup may be filled to the brim in this life so to speak, but I know you have a "wild witch hair" story somewhere. Perhaps you're a little lonely in your Norman Rockwell painting. Maybe you've suppressed your deepest longings so that your husband could excel. You wouldn't dare speak up because "that's not what Christian women do," or because that wasn't the dynamic you had in your childhood home. If this is you, it's time. Maybe you're ridiculously shy—so shy that you feel awkward and clam up in a crowd. You may have loved your home as a young child so much because you could color and play quietly or perhaps you wish you were more fun around other people. You may sing to your heart's content in the shower, but you're petrified of even clapping outside your home. It's time for all of us to embrace our wiring. It's time to let go of the person you want to be or think you should be and become who God actually created you to be. It's time you looked societal norms in the face and spit on them. It's time you tell the noise where it can go. Life isn't meant to be lived in a box. Or by a checklist. Or scripted. Or the same as everyone else. You are uniquely and intentionally designed! It's time we believe the words of King David in Psalm 139:

I praise you, for I am fearfully and wonderfully made. Wonderful are your works; my soul knows it very well.

Psalm 139:14 (ESV)

Sister, does your soul know it?

Not long ago, a family member called to tell me that a dear friend of ours was diagnosed with cancer. As you can imagine, the news was devastating. After she told me about the diagnosis, she went on to tell me what to say to her. She told me not to be loud. She reminded me that this was a hard time for our friend and that I needed to act a certain way and say certain things to her. This went on for a good five minutes and the more she told me how to react, the more I felt put back in my box. The conversation triggered my "wild witch hair" memory and reminded me how different I am. When we hung up, I cried. Was I so embarrassing that I needed a script to comfort a friend? Am I a burden to people when they're suffering? Why do I need to be shushed? Do I always say the wrong thing? Am I ridiculous? Do you have a story like this? A situation where you feel unheard? Unseen? Silenced? Ridiculous? Do you ever feel like you're being told to calm down or to pep up? If so, I'm sorry. From the bottom of my soul, I'm sorry, because I know it hurts.

This time, as my tears fell, something different happened. Instead of cueing the violin, I listened to Jesus. And do you know what he told me that day? He told me to be "Kim" for this person. He told me to be loud, to show emotion, to expose my feelings in a raw, authentic way because that was the superpower he gave me. I used to think it was a bad thing to be loud and undignified. And y'all, it can be. If I am attention-seeking to the point of needing affirmation or if I am obsessing over my appearance, then obviously that's wrong. But if I'm being loud in an attempt to point people to Jesus, God told me to bring it. He reminded me to be undignified in his name, much like King David. Do you remember his half-naked dancing story? The one where David was praising the Lord and dancing to his heart's content—only he was half naked? But here's the thing. David wasn't shaking his hips to show off. There were no "Moves Like Jagger." He wasn't performing or trying to be noticed. Nope, he was being loud for his Savior! He didn't feel the need to bring his fancy clothes and act like a king. He didn't feel the need to bring his dignity or title, even after his wife Michal tried to box him in.

David returned home to bless his family. Michal, Saul's daughter, came out to greet him: "How wonderfully the king has distinguished himself today—exposing himself to the eyes of the servants' maids like some burlesque street dancer!" David replied to Michal, "In God's presence I'll dance all I want! He chose me over your father and the rest of our family and made me prince over God's people, over Israel. Oh yes, I'll dance to God's glory—more recklessly even than this. And as far as I'm concerned . . . I'll gladly look like a fool . . . but among these maids you're so worried about, I'll be honored no end."

2 Samuel 6:20–22 (MSG)

Sister, dance like David. Dance "to God's glory more recklessly even than this." Do not let some hater or even someone who loves you put you in a box not meant for you. As long as you're pointing people to Jesus, you have his blessing to scream of his goodness—or if you're quiet, to whisper of his goodness. No human being on this planet gets to tell you who you are. Never. Ever. Ever. Sadly, I have walked into rooms where I've consciously told myself to be as quiet as possible. I literally thought, *Do not be yourself. You're too much. You're intense. People think you're weird. Stop talking.* Sister, where's your faulty thinking? What box do you feel put in? What box do you put yourself in? Do you walk into a room and want to disappear? Do you second-guess everything you say? Do you think you're so ugly that you're afraid to speak because someone may actually look at you? Do you think you have nothing to bring? Do you think you're dumb? Do you think you're too smart and will come off as a know-it-all? What kind of garbage do you find yourself thinking? Whatever it is, name it. Say it out loud. Here's mine: I'm extra. I talk loudly. I write in all caps. I tell everyone I love them, even the plumber. I'm wild and energetic. And as long as I am pointing people to Jesus, I don't need to be any different—I don't want to calm down!

No human being on this planet
gets to tell you who you are.

Listen to me: you don't need to calm down. It would be denying the world your God-given gifts to be any different than the way he made you. You are his design. His perfect craftsmanship. You were thought of in your mother's womb. So, I'll ask you again: What gift are you sitting on out of insecurity? Because let me tell you something. That inner critic you hear isn't logic. And it certainly is not God. That's Satan's voice you are hearing, and he dances "the floss" when you act on his faulty logic. He absolutely wants you to "calm down." Your unwavering loyalty, your steady friendship, your discerning spirit, your prayerful manner. He wants you to sit on those gifts because they are a threat to him. He will use your insecurity, your husband, your busyness, your kids, all of it to distract you from your God-given purpose. Recognize that Satan is after you like white on rice because you are a threat to him. There is not any role on this earth more important than bringing glory to Jesus, and Satan hates that. He will do anything to distract you from this purpose. And I mean anything. He will deflate you. He will keep you busy with less important things. He will make you comfortable. He will whisper lies into your ear. Anything. Stay alert.

I wish we could grab a cup of coffee so I could shake your shoulders and scream, "Be you!" Be the best version of you because my stars you are as unique as a snowflake. That sounds so cheesy, I know, but did you know that not one snowflake is alike? Pretty cool, but for real, if your motive is to point people to Jesus then be all in. Give it your all and be undignified. Maybe you're really smart. Maybe you're an artist. Maybe you're discerning. Maybe you're a good listener. Or maybe you're bold and loud like me. Whatever it is, do it, be it, own it in Jesus' name. Don't water yourself down so others can tolerate you.

It's really hard to be yourself, I know. There are so many competing voices telling us who to be. The world has so many expectations of us. Honestly, the church itself has expectations of us, but here's the deal: Jesus alone gets to set the tone. He gets to tell us what to do and who to be. So, how do we hear his voice? Good question. And I'm going to give you the church answer. By praying and reading his Word. It's really that simple.

There are so many great sources feeding our souls, so many outlets telling you what you should or shouldn't be doing with your life—who you should or shouldn't be. "Do more of this." "Do less of that." But here's the deal. If you can't find scripture to back up what you're hearing, toss it. The Bible is literally the only truth. Not your pastor. Not some godly lady you follow on Instagram. Not some book you are reading *about* the Bible. Certainly not me. No, girl—the Bible. Television, Pinterest, social media, celebrities—everyone is trying to influence you. But everything you read, watch, or listen to should be measured next to the Bible. It is your litmus test for truth. Any person, Christian or not, who feeds you a different message is not basing their claims on truth. I've had to put down countless books that have tweaked Scripture ever so slightly in attempts to justify culture—books that redefined marriage. Books that changed the way to salvation or renamed sexuality. Hear me loud and clear as I say this: there is no Jesus plus anything—only Jesus. I plead with you not to open the door to such heresy. It can ruin you. Please, please, please hear me when I say this: read your Bible.

I say this in love. I say this with urgency. I say this as someone who barely read her Bible until not that long ago. I say this as someone who used to find the Bible boring. You are not a "bad" Christian if you find the Bible boring or intimidating. Take that off the table now. For the longest time I would read the Bible and wait to be moved. I would read a few lines and forget what I read and have to start over. I'd go through seasons where I wouldn't even read the Bible. If this is you, then, please know that you are not alone. Speak up. Tell someone that you are struggling with reading the Bible. There are so many resources out there to help: Bible reading plans, groups, people who can hold you accountable and help you understand. Y'all, there is a community of people who feel just like you do. I am one of those people! Not really knowing how or being motivated to read the Bible is actually pretty normal—and human.

The other life-giver to our souls is **community**. Don't roll your eyes. This is nonnegotiable for healthy living. And before you start with the "buts," I'm going to stop you now. This is not an introvert-versus-extrovert debate. I also don't want to hear that you're too busy to have friends or go deep with people. Jesus did not put a disclaimer in the Bible for specific personalities. He did not build his church with a specific Enneagram number in mind. While individual leanings shape the way community looks for each person, it does not give you a pass from vulnerability and accountability. Jesus modeled this when he chose twelve disciples to do life with. You can't be "all in" with your ten thousand social media followers—or your coworkers—or your college friends you keep up with every few months. Your community is your tribe. They are the people you do life with. They pray with you. They break bread with you. They worship with you. They push you to Jesus. So, find your tribe. Find your people, whether it's two or fifty, and do life with them. Love the mess out of them. Be vulnerable with them. Proverbs 27:17 says it perfectly:

Iron sharpens iron, and one man sharpens another.

Proverbs 27:17 (ESV)

Cultural messages are loud and not anchored in truth. They are sneaky and in your face. I feel like every time I look at my phone, I'm being told to be something different. *"Be loud." "Be quiet." "Be pretty." "Be healthy." "Be independent." "Be in need." "You only live once (YOLO)." "Want for nothing."* It's exhausting, and I'd be lying if I didn't admit to you that I'm overwhelmed by it all. But I do know this. You have to be you. That's not code for complacency. That's absolutely not an excuse to remain unchanged. It's simply encouragement to be the best version of yourself. So, whether loud and proud or confidently quiet, allow the God who created you in his image to show off his glory with the gifts he gave you.

Before I shaped you in the womb, I knew all about you. Before you saw the light of day, I had holy plans for you...

Jeremiah 1:5a (MSG)

3

Sister, find it.

*The woman who does not require
validation from anyone is the most
feared individual on the planet.*

Mohadesa Najumi

SOMEBODY SAID SOMETHING to me the other day and it was crushing. *"Your energy is exhausting. I can't stand to have you in my presence because you're so draining."* Y'all, this gutted me. What this woman said was meant to be mean. It was meant to crush my soul, and it did just that. Her words were cruel, yes, but they did more than hurt my feelings. They exposed me. They played on my deepest insecurity. They zeroed in smack dab on my innermost struggle, a struggle I've wrestled with my entire life: the struggle of being "too much."

We all have that one thing we really struggle with. I'm not talking about your big butt or your crooked nose. I'm talking about that one part of who you are that you just aren't sure about. It could be that you're shy—so shy that you want to disappear. You know you need to speak up, to be known, but you are frozen in fear. Or maybe you don't think you're smart or talented enough. Or worthy. Maybe you don't feel you belong. Whatever it is, we all have something, and if not put in check, this "one thing" will paralyze you.

I've always struggled with my intensity. My tenacity. My zeal. The words "you're too much" and "calm down" haunt me. Many, many times I've questioned the way God wired me. Does anyone else do that? Does anyone else have the audacity to ask the God who created the universe why he made you the way you are? Have you ever expressed to God, the very one who breathed life into you, all of your self-doubts? *"God, why am I so (fill in the blank)? Why am I so awkward? So stupid? Not good enough?"* I've spent a lot of time soul-searching this one. Honestly, I've flat out wanted to be different. Even now it has a tendency to be a struggle. Even as I write this, knowing the beauty in God's design for each one of us, knowing how God can use every one of his children—knowing that he wants me to tell you to embrace who you are, I struggle. And when I struggle, there's always a psalm to breathe life into my soul:

For you formed my inward parts; you knitted me together in my mother's womb. I praise you, for I am fearfully and wonderfully made. Wonderful are your works; my soul knows it very well.

Psalm 139:13–14 (ESV)

Yet here I am, still longing to be more compliant with the crowd. The truth is, I've always held back a little for fear of being truly known. Sometimes I'm scared to be the real me, scared to show how intensely I feel the hurts of this world. Scared to tell my husband how very much he means to me. Scared to admit that someone's words hurt me to the core. Scared to embrace the calling God has for me, all for fear of rejection. Tell me I'm not alone here. Tell me that you, too, hear the noise. The noise of the world. The noise of your humanity. The noise that comes from hell. Because, y'all, the noise is loud, and it's constant.

"Be compliant. No, be a mover and a shaker."
"Be assertive. No, be more subservient."
"Be courageous. No, stay in your box."
"Be bold. No, calm down."
"Be confident. No, be humble."
"Be loud. No, quit having an opinion."
"Be healthy. No, be skinny."
"Be generous. No, be frugal."

Do you hear it too? The constant contradictions? I feel like I'm wired one way, but the noise tells me to be something else. I feel like I want to do one thing, but I'm expected to do something else. The *noise* is overwhelming, so overwhelming at times that it's tempting to pull the covers over my head and just freeze. So overwhelming it's easier to just play along. So overwhelming it's easier to suppress that still small voice in the midst of the noise. You know the voice I'm talking about: that steadfast, confident voice that tells you who you are. The voice that makes everything okay.

In the midst of your questioning, in the midst of your spiraling, *you know his voice.* In the midst of the false information you're being fed, there's a voice speaking life into your soul. A voice that says, "you're mine." A voice that says, "I want you. I chose you. I died for you." A voice that says, "I created you to be exactly the way you are." That voice—that's the voice your soul needs to hone in on, because *that* voice is the voice of the one who had you in mind when he created the universe. And that voice tells you that the only approval that matters is his. That voice reminds you that you have nothing to prove.

For they loved human praise more than the praise of God.

John 12:43 (NLT)

Remember in my introduction where I said I was willing to completely expose myself if it would help you to wake up? This verse, and the truth that God is the only audience I should care about, is a tough one for me, so let me lay out my sin for you here. So many of the "godly" things I do come with selfish intentions. I have always been an advocate at heart—so much so that I became a social worker. I work with the oppressed and those in need. Fighting for injustice comes naturally to me. Sadly, however, when I do kind things for people, part of me has an ulterior motive. You see, I want to be thought of as good. I want to be loved. And the honest truth is that my natural tendency is to be an insecure people pleaser that does things for a high five from humanity. Oftentimes, I find my motives are not always rooted in Jesus. I crave a fist bump from my boss. I long for my dad to be proud of me. I ache for my husband to approve of me. I crave the applause of others for my parenting skills or for my children.

Sometimes the approval I seek from people is in sync with the approval I seek from God. I mean, sometimes the "right thing" also pleases God in theory, but—he knows our hearts. He knows when we seek human approval over his, and we know it too. Proverbs 16:2 says:

> *All the ways of a man are pure in his own eyes, but the Lord weighs the spirit.*
>
> Proverbs 16:2 (ESV)

For some reason, God's approval is not always enough for me. I want the cheap, instant gratification that comes from the verbal praise of man. And call me crazy, but I don't think I'm alone here. Think about the last kind, generous, or sacrificial thing you did. Did you do it out of obligation? Did you do it because you couldn't bring yourself to say no? Did you do it so that someone would see how great you are? Did you do it because it made you feel good? While these reasons are not bad in and of themselves, they're not godly. I don't care who it is; when you seek the approval of anyone other than Jesus Christ, that approval becomes the god you serve.

Maybe you say yes to every ministry opportunity not because the Spirit moves you but because you want to be accepted. Maybe you work out and diet because you think your worth is measured by the number you see on the scale or how you look in your jeans. Maybe you seek validation from your parents before you make a decision. You're a grown woman, maybe even married, yet your parents' seal of approval matters in every decision you make. Maybe you stay home when you really want to work because you fear mom shame.

> **When you seek the approval of anyone other than Jesus Christ, that approval becomes the god you serve.**

Y'all, this stuff is insane! All of it! And if we're not careful, we will lose sight of Jesus, even in our seemingly "good" pursuits. In all of our harmless acts of looking cute, working out, and heading every church committee, we can easily lose our way if our intentions are about us or the approval of others. First Corinthians 10 tells us it's all about motive:

So, whether you eat or drink, or whatever you do, do all to the glory of God.

1 Corinthians 10:31 (ESV)

I'm not saying we should read our Bibles all day long, but my stars, this verse tells us that we need to do *everything* with Jesus in mind. We should exercise for the glory of God. We should serve for the glory of God. We should eat for the glory of God! Nothing, and I mean nothing, should be done for the glory of man. The scary thing is that we often don't even realize our motives are misplaced; we have grown numb to our hearts. Some of us are in such bondage to seeking approval that we no longer even recognize it. We live our lives on autopilot, walking around with our empty "approval" cups, hoping someone or something will fill it to the brim. In a world that takes selfies, that competes on social media, in a world that tells you what you should be, remember who you are. God wired each of us uniquely and strategically for his purpose. *His* purpose, y'all. That means he gave you your traits and leanings with a path designed specifically for you. You are a unique individual who has been given the incredible opportunity to display the glory of a great God. In no way, shape, or form does Scripture tell us that we deserve a high five. Nor does it tell us that we need someone else's approval. These words are very sobering for a girl who still calls her mom when her cup is empty. In fact, Galatians 1 says:

For am I now seeking the approval of man, or of God? Or am I trying to please man? If I were still trying to please man, I would not be a servant of Christ.

Galatians 1:10 (ESV)

An "approval" cup full to the brim will never be enough if you are a servant of Christ. You can't please both God and man. You just can't.

Hear me loud and clear when I say this next part: your mother is not enough. Your husband is not enough. Your job is not enough. Your amazing body is not enough. Your wealth is not enough. Your success is not enough. Words, things, people, they are not enough to satisfy our insatiable appetites for approval. Why? Because you will never get the approval you need from the world. In Psalm 42, King David states:

As a deer pants for flowing streams, so pants my soul for you, O God.
Psalm 42:1 (ESV)

Listen, David had everything the world craves. He had wealth, prosperity, success, women. But guess what? It wasn't enough for him, and he knew that. People turned on him. His family life was a mess. Wealth and prosperity couldn't sustain him in those dark moments. He was desperate for God like a deer is thirsty for water. Jesus himself said in John 5:41 (MSG), *"I'm not interested in crowd approval."* Jesus understood his own deep need for God's approval. In fact, he understood this so well that he never wavered, even in front of a large crowd. Even when questioned by his friends. Even when he was dying on the cross. Jesus knew he only needed God to smile upon him. Listen, unless we chase only after God's approval the way Jesus modeled for us so perfectly, we will be on a wild goose chase for our entire lives.

I would love to have the confidence of not caring about other people's opinions, but I'm a people pleaser in recovery—and I am certain I will be in recovery all my life. In fact, I ache for approval the way an alcoholic aches for a drink. In small ways, in big ways—I want it. I crave it. But this is not the way we were created to live. And, oh, my stars, let's just call it what it truly is: insecurity, the sinful little sister of pride. The obsessing, the constant analyzing: this is all unnecessary. Here is the truth: if the Lord is at the root of all you do, some coworker's opinion of you shouldn't shake your foundation. If the Lord is your compass, your social media following shouldn't matter. If you are anchored in Jesus, knowing you are obedient to him is enough. Remember: no matter how perfect you are, "haters gonna hate." (Thank you, Taylor Swift.)

Can you imagine the freedom of a steady hand when opposition arises? Can you imagine the freedom of not obsessing about an argument because it was handled humbly and in love? Can you imagine the freedom of walking in truth and being so anchored in who God says you are that an insensitive family member's opinion doesn't even penetrate? Can you imagine the freedom in being so rooted in Jesus that your scale no longer defines you? I equate this to driving in a Jeep with my hair blowing in the wind, radio turned up loud, sunshine on my face—that kind of freedom. Gosh, I want this. I want this so much. Who is with me?

> ***If we don't chase only after God's approval the way Jesus modeled for us so perfectly, we will be on a wild goose chase for our entire lives.***

So, what does this even look like? How do we get this kind of freedom? The bad news is that I don't have all the answers. Not even close. But as a people pleaser (in recovery) I can tell you what I know to be true with every fiber of my being. Reading God's word is nonnegotiable. And it's most often best to start your day off with him. Why? Because most human beings I know look at their social media accounts first thing in the morning. Don't get me wrong. I love social media, but it has a sneaky way of trying to tell you who you are. I don't think it means to, but it attempts to tell you your worth. And more often than not, it has the potential to scream that you aren't enough. I mean, look at that girl from church who is having coffee on her screened-in porch in her nice house. Or that girl from high school who lives in the big city and is living the life you always wanted. Or the girl who has already worked out and made her kids' breakfast when you're rolling out of bed at 7:00 a.m. with a sugar hangover. Feeling unworthy and not good enough is not how you want to start your day. Hear me when I say this. Social media is dangerous without being anchored in truth. In fact, I'd go as far as to say that you shouldn't even look at it if you aren't actively in God's Word. There's just not enough balance, and without weighing it next to truth, the deception will engulf you.

I'm going to say this as emphatically as I can: ***We all bring something different to the kingdom***. All of us. If you don't believe me, then believe the Word of God. Ephesians 2:10 says:

> *For we are his workmanship, created in Christ Jesus for good works, which God prepared beforehand, that we should walk in them.*
>
> Ephesians 2:10 (ESV)

You hear that? We were *prepared beforehand* to do great things for him. That means that we were not created simply to suck oxygen or to take up space. We weren't created to add to the pollution problem. No. We actually have a purpose. So, find it. If you don't know how to find it, ask a friend or a counselor or a minister. Find it. Own it. Own your spiritual gifts. Own your wiring. Own your leanings. Bring the weird. Bring the loud. Bring the shy. Bring the creative. Bring the awkward. And do me a favor. Don't you dare apologize when you bring it. As long as you're pointing people to Jesus, you have his permission and blessing to bring it.

I am not responsible to the person who told me that my energy is exhausting. I am responsible only for me, for using the gifts God gave me. That loud and audacious voice that exhausts her? It's my superpower given to me by Jesus Christ. And if I'm glorifying the Lord with my loud, audacious self, then someone's disapproval of me shouldn't even matter. Now I'm asking you: what is your superpower? Are you creative? Do you have a discerning spirit? Can you write? Are you a servant? Are you a born leader? Are you a prayer warrior? Whatever it is, own it. Be it loud and proud. Color outside the lines with it. Give it all you got—with vigor, with a big red bow and a cherry on top. Serve *him*, not to elevate your own importance. Sing for *him*, not to be seen and appreciated. Work for *him*, not to be wealthy. Whatever your gift, use it for his glory and go wild with it, knowing that you have the approval of the one who matters—not that of your boss, not your mom or dad, not even your husband.

Truth is, you will make people mad. Your loved ones will shake their heads when you fail to meet their expectations. You will be too much. You won't be enough. But here's the deal: your job isn't to meet everyone else's expectations. Your job is to be like Jesus. Your job isn't to convince people of who you are. The Lord tells you who you are. Just because people don't get you doesn't mean there's something wrong with you, and it most certainly doesn't mean you should change. No, girl. Let your hair down. Turn the music up and be the girl God had in mind when he knit you together perfectly in your mother's womb. You owe it to yourself. You owe it to the people you will serve. And most of all, you owe it to the one who died for you.

Let every detail in your lives—words, actions, whatever—be done in the name of the Master, Jesus, thanking God the Father every step of the way.

Colossians 3:17 (MSG)

4

Sister, move!

You're not a tree. So, move;
make something happen.
Richelle E. Goodrich

I HATE THE SAYING "It is what it is." To me it sounds like a reason not to face the gravity of a situation. It's almost like giving yourself a pass. The other day someone told me she hates her job, complaining she makes no money. "No one is hiring. I have applied for every job in the city." Then she said, "It is what it is." *"Really?"* I wanted to say. "You have applied for *every* job in the entire city? *No* one is hiring? Have you *prayed* about it? Have you done any networking?" I wanted to tell her she was being ridiculous, that she has done nothing but whine about the situation, but I zipped it. I shut my pie hole while wanting so badly to scream, "No, girl. It is *not* what it is."

But I'm not without a soul, though sometimes I feel like I come off that way. A dear friend told recently that she was about to start radiation and chemo for a tumor in her uterus. I was so broken for her. The doctors were pretty sure this would prevent her from having more kids and, for a while, from working. Her husband was in school and her income was all they had. The whole thing was a nightmare. After she told me, I went to her house to pray with her. I showed up with ice cream and about three different books to pass on to her. I had verses on pain and suffering.

I was ready to be there for her. After sharing her painful situation with me, she wiped her tears and said those five dreaded words: "It is what it is." Truth? As much as I wanted to throw cold water on her face, I know why she said it. In fact, I know why most people say, "It is what it is." I think deep down, whether we realize it or not, we're trying to cover for God. I know, gasp! I said it. I mean, who would ever think that we need to make excuses for almighty God?

Well, for starters, me—and maybe you too. Think about it. Our prayers don't seem to be answered the way we had hoped—or at all. We start to doubt. Time passes. We feel very little change in our situation, yet the church girl in us would never admit that God appears to have gone radio silent. That's too irreverent, right? So we coast. We slap an "It is what it is" on our situation and do our best to go through the motions, all the while thinking maybe God isn't real. Or maybe that God isn't good. Or maybe that you're not really a Christian for thinking these things. I know the audacity in thinking this way. It's faulty thinking, for sure, but sometimes it does feel this way. Many of us, when faced with adversity, are scared that God *isn't* good, that he doesn't really answer our prayers—that maybe we aren't really saved. Some of you may take these feelings to the grave. And I get that. It's pretty embarrassing and irreverent, but I will admit that I still feel like this sometimes. And I think you might too. And if you don't, then chances are your daughter or friend or sister in Christ is feeling this. There is power in recognizing our doubts because, once you spot this tendency in yourself, you can face reality with Jesus by your side. You can fight the natural instinct to become complacent. To give up. To go numb. To gloss over your deep hurts. You can unfreeze. Face your hurts. Be brave. And make changes. Just ask Peter.

Remember Peter in the Bible? He's kind of my favorite. He followed the Lord imperfectly, yes, but, oh, so recklessly. Remember the story about Jesus walking on the water in Matthew 14? If not, allow me to refresh you. The disciples are asleep on a fishing boat and wake to finding Jesus walking on the water. They were petrified, of course, so they start screaming stuff like, "It's a ghost!" Jesus assures them he's not a ghost and tells them to chill—in a very nice way, of course. Here's where my guy Peter comes in. He asks God to call him to the water. Man, I love his audacity. If we could only be so bold. If we could ask God to invite us to the water. To the extraordinary. Out of our complacency. Out of our "it is what it is" thinking. Out of the false security of the boat.

Peter gets out of the boat and starts walking toward Jesus. On the water, if you will. At some point he looks down and starts to freak out. He begins to sink and cries out. Jesus saves him, of course. It's an amazing story, but here's what's applicable to us. Peter got out of the boat! He was the only disciple brave enough to try. He was the only one of these godly men who had the courage to ask Jesus for a front row seat to awesomeness. He was the only one willing to lean in to his discomfort. And fear. All the other guys were comfy and cozy in their safe place. I'm not knocking them. In fact, I relate to them. Comfort is always easier. Glossing over issues and hurts? Yes, please. I have a reserved seat in this section. Unfortunately, it's the nosebleed section. Courtside seats involve getting out of the boat, but they are the best seats in the house.

> *Many of us, when faced with adversity, are scared that God isn't good, that he doesn't really answer our prayers—that maybe we aren't really saved.*

Some of you may have heard this phrase, but for those of you who haven't, allow me to elaborate. When I say "get out of the boat," this is a very personal and tailored action step for each of us. Everybody's walk on water is going to be something different. It could mean something seemingly small or something huge. That's between you and the Lord but, for the record, there is no "small." But our reaction to whatever it is, big or small, should be the same. When God nudges us out of our comfort zone, our boat, we pray and hike our leg over. It may be shaky, but we do it. We take a step. We may be afraid, but we do it anyway. Pay attention to this next part because this is where Peter messed up. He looked down. He looked at all the hard things. He looked at all the barriers. He looked at all the reasons why he shouldn't be stepping out of the boat. He doubted. Peter took his eyes off Jesus. *This* moment. This is the moment where he could have slapped an "it is what it is" on the situation. He could have just assumed that greatness was not on the other side. He could have thought like everyone else. He could have stayed on the boat like everyone else. He could have returned to the boat. But he didn't.

And you shouldn't either. Why? Because when Peter was sinking, Jesus reached out his hand for him. He saved him. Just like he will save you.

The calling from the water. Girl, the calling is hard and sometimes lonely. It may seem so small to the outside world. Your closest people may not understand. It may be that you're a shy girl showing up to a Bible study where you know no one. It may be that God wants you to break up with someone you love who is not right for you. It may be that he wants you to take a step to a healthier lifestyle or mindset. Like my friend, it may be that he wants you to face an unknown prognosis. Listen, callings are equally scary. There's no comparison here. They all require something from us. Discomfort. Vulnerability. Rejection. And that inner critic you hear telling you it's not worth the hassle, that this is not the season to do this. That things are fine the way they are. Y'all, that's not God speaking; that's Satan. And Satan wants you to stay on the boat. He hates you. He doesn't want you to be extraordinary. He doesn't want you to walk on water. He wants you to stay comfy and cozy and afraid.

"But I'm stuck."

"This is too hard."

"Nothing good ever happens to me."

"Someone else is already doing it."

"I'm too busy."

"What if I fail?"

Do you know what kills me? I mean "nails on the chalkboard" drives me crazy? People who stay stuck. People who don't try. People who whine. People who live in mediocrity when they don't have to. I understand the process is excruciating. I understand the hesitation. But here's the honest truth. You can't stay paused forever. Life is not supposed to suck. God did not send his one and only son to die so you can walk around hating your life. The Lord did not die for you so you can stay in the boat and coast. Sure, there are hard seasons. There are many hard seasons where you will be paralyzed, where you will sit in pain, where you will sit in less than desirable moments, but we can't stay here forever. God doesn't want us to stay here forever.

Here's the part where I might make you mad. Here's my call to action on your life. Please don't mistake it for judgment. Please know I'm challenging you in attempts to sober you up. Daughter of Jesus, beloved: you have a brain. You have a mind. You have two hands and two feet. You live in an educated society. This is not seventeenth-century America. You have rights. You have opportunities. You have choices. You have health care. You have more than most people in the world. And you have the Bible. Stop saying, "I'll pray for God to get me out of this," while you sit there waiting to be rescued. Stop asking God to send a life raft when he's already provided you with everything you need. Listen to Peter:

> *By his divine power, God has given us everything we need for living a godly life.*
>
> 2 Peter 1:3a (NLT)

Stop listing all the reasons you *can't* do this or that, and hear his voice simply asking you to *come*. Get counseling. Get support. Get what you need, but *come*.

"But you don't know my circumstances," you say to excuse yourself. "I have health issues." "My husband limits me." "I'm poor." "I'm not smart." "Someone else is already doing what I want to do." "I have small kids." Sisters, I am in no way saying you can change everything. We all have things that we can't change and have to accept. For example, my sister has a child with autism. She can't change that. My dear friend has lupus. There are literally seasons where she can't get out of bed. These are things that will not change. But there are so many things that we *can* change. You hate your job? Okay. Let's talk about this. I once had a friend tell me that her job is just a paycheck. I am in no way questioning her lack of passion for her work because that was enough for her in that season. But, that is not enough for me right now. If I am taking my kids to "parents' day out" or day care, if I miss meeting the school bus in the afternoon because I'm at work, if I have to put on a dang bra and makeup on the daily, I had better be using my gifts. Because, y'all, we won't be happy if we are not using our gifts. It doesn't have to necessarily be at work, but living out the way God wired us for his glory with the gifts he has given us is nonnegotiable for abundant living. God created you with a distinctive set of gifts, those things that get your heart pumping. Those gifts are unique to you. Breathe life into them in Jesus' name!

Stop asking God to send a life raft when he's already provided you with everything you need.

———

Stop listing all the reasons you can't, and hear his voice simply asking you to come.

———

"But I'm a single mom," you might say. "I need the income of this job that I hate." Okay, cool. Keep your job for now. Keep making an incredible paycheck. But hike your leg over the boat and look to Jesus while you look for something else. You want to be an artist but can't because you have to be an adult. Cool. Paint on the side. Paint after hours until you can do it as often as you like. You want to write. Awesome. Start writing. Write on social media. Start a blog. I don't mean to sound so hard core. I get the struggle. I get the insecurity of it all. I get that self-starting is hard. Changing habits and old patterns is the hardest. Vulnerability is tough. It's overwhelming. But it's why I love Peter! He struggled. He was scared, but, still, he got out of the boat. We have to get out of the boat too.

I feel like now is the perfect opportunity for me to tell you about a group of people that make me very sad. You know who they are. You may even be one. And the sad thing is that if you are one of these people, you probably don't realize it. They are the navel-gazers of the world. I used to think that was a made-up word, but it is a for-real thing. Navel-gazers are people who are so into their own problems that they miss everything going on around them. They are focused only on the one issue right in front of them and miss the bigger picture. They literally stare down at their navels in sadness and miss the beauty of life happening in front of them. They miss the joys of life. The things they can change. They have their head down so low they literally stare at their belly buttons. Debbie Downers they are often called. Have you been around somebody like that? They are usually very negative. And draining. There's always an excuse as to why they can't change. Now that we have learned a new word, let me ask you this: Are you a navel-gazer? If the answer is yes, take heart! There's hope. The Bible is full of redemptive stories of navel-gazers. My favorite is Naomi.

Have you heard of her? She's the mother-in-law to Ruth in the Bible. Allow me to refresh you on this beautifully redemptive story tucked in the Old Testament in the book of Ruth. Naomi's husband dies. She also has two sons who both die. Even worse, they both die before they can give her grandbabies. Obviously, this is very sad in itself, but back in that time, having a lineage and a man to protect you was everything. Naomi now has none of these things. I'm telling you, this was not the era in which we live. She didn't have the option of starting a company or becoming an influencer and being an overcomer. This is basically a death sentence for her. She begs her daughters-in-law to leave her behind. This sounds noble, but this is where you can cue the violin. She's basically telling them, "My life sucks. Move on. Save yourself. I'm of no use to you." She even changes her name to Mara because it means "bitter." Her exact words in Ruth 1 are:

> *Do not call me Naomi; call me Mara, for the Almighty has dealt very bitterly with me.*
>
> Ruth 1:20b (ESV)

Talk about navel-gazing! But that's where she was. I've sure been there.

One of her daughters-in-law takes her up on her offer and "peace outs." The other one, Ruth, stays. They go to Bethlehem, and Ruth ends up marrying Boaz and births Obed. Stay with me here for this next part. Obed is in the direct lineage of Jesus. He is King David's grandfather. So many cool things are happening here. First of all, Ruth was critical to Naomi's recovery from navel-gazing. She was loyal, patient, strong, and kind. Naomi couldn't have survived, much less overcome her situation and her grief without Ruth's loving commitment to her. But God was also using Naomi, even when she was paralyzed by her grief. You see, Ruth would not have connected with Boaz without Naomi's intervention. It was this intervention that allowed Naomi to take her eyes off herself, and, oh, my gosh, look up from that navel of hers!

Please go read the short but redemptive story of Naomi and Ruth on your own. It ends with Naomi wrapping her arms around her grandson and taking care of him the rest of her days. Redemption is so beautiful. Naomi had been *gazing downward*. She was in pain. She was grieving. She was sad and felt hopeless. But God is always working behind the scenes. He is right there with you. Don't slap an "it is what it is" on your pain. Don't coast. And, for the love, don't navel-gaze.

While there is no shelf life on grief, there will be a time to get up and work through the pain. I won't even begin to put a label on what the process should look like for you or attempt to give you a time frame for your situation. Everybody gets the grace to mourn in their own way and in their own time. Everyone's pain looks different too. Some of our pain is acute. It may stem from a situation that gets easier over time. Some of our pain, however, is chronic. As in it always remains. In fact, it may never get better this side of heaven, but stay with me here. I'm not sure that's a bad thing. I know I sound all Mary Sunshine, but from an eternal perspective this is everything! You see, pain keeps you close to God. It keeps you depending on him every minute of every day. It really gives you an opportunity to know Jesus. I mean really know him. And guess what else? It has meaning. Every second of your pain matters in glory. Your suffering is not in vain. It has a purpose. It's doing something. I know this doesn't always keep you feeling warm and fuzzy when you're struggling so badly you want to die. I know the days are long when life is hard. I know. But I pray that knowing that your situation matters and is making a difference eternally will keep you from being controlled by it. And guess what the icing on the cake is? Nothing can separate you from the love of God. Nothing. Just ask Paul, who wrote in Romans 8:

> *Can anything ever separate us from Christ's love? Does it mean he no longer loves us if we have trouble or calamity, or are persecuted, or hungry, or destitute, or in danger, or threatened with death? (As the Scriptures say, "For your sake we are killed every day; we are being slaughtered like sheep.") No, despite all these things, overwhelming victory is ours through Christ, who loved us. And I am convinced that nothing can ever separate us from God's love. Neither death nor life, neither angels nor demons, neither our fears for today nor our worries about tomorrow—not even the powers of hell can separate us from God's love. No power in the sky above or in the earth below—indeed, nothing in all creation will ever be able to separate us from the love of God that is revealed in Christ Jesus our Lord.*
>
> Romans 8:35–39 (NLT)

Sister, don't be conquered by your hardships; be a conqueror. I don't care if you are eighteen or eighty. I don't care if you've sat in your pain for three days or thirty years. It's not too late for you to lift your gaze and return to him. The book of Joel says:

'Yet even now,' declares the LORD, 'return to me with all your heart, with fasting, with weeping, and with mourning.'

Joel 2:12 (ESV)

Even now. Throw a leg over the boat and walk to Jesus. He's waiting.

Finally, be strong in the Lord and in the strength of his might.

Ephesians 6:10 (ESV)

5

Sister, cut it off!

*I want you to give up the one thing you
crave more than me. Then come follow Me.*

Lysa Terkuerst

THE OTHER DAY I was teaching first graders about the rich
young ruler in the Bible. Do you remember that story? It's found
in Matthew 19:16–30, Mark 10:17–22, and Luke 18:18–23. It's
actually pretty tragic. A rich man comes up to Jesus and asks him what
he can do to have eternal life. After checking the "I follow the Ten Commandments" box, Jesus takes it one step further. He tells the man to sell
everything he has and give the proceeds to the poor. Only then, he says,
could the man can follow him. Upon hearing this, the man's face falls
and he walks away, tail between his legs. This story blows my mind every
time I read it. The dude is staring Jesus Christ in the face, but he can't let
go of his possessions. His wealth. His success. His comfort. And because
he can't, it costs him his soul. Before you deduce this man to be an idiot,
let me interject that I relate to the rich young ruler, and I think you do
too. For the most part, I follow the Ten Commandments. I don't get
wasted. I don't lie on my taxes. I go to church. I read my Bible. Seriously,
Ten Commandments—check. But here is where Jesus goes too far.

Be generous. Give to the poor.

Luke 12:33a (MSG)

Or does he? For decades I've glossed over this text. "It's not like I have anything that precious to sell," I've told myself for years. "I don't live in a mansion. I don't drive a Ferrari. I don't have designer anything. We don't take lavish vacations. I am nothing like the rich young ruler." Well, here's where I was wrong. And if you think this story doesn't apply to you, I want you to insert your own kryptonite as I ask you a question. What is it you crave more than Jesus?

I'll ask it another way. What is it Jesus wants you to give up in order to truly follow him? It may be something temporary. Something he asks you to refrain from for a season. Or it may be a god you've come to worship. I want you to really think about this. And if you're struggling to pinpoint what exactly it is, start with comfort. Instead of selling possessions, imagine Jesus saying: "Daughter, I want you to stop filling your emptiness by buying all the things at Target and on Amazon. Then, come follow me. Daughter, I want you to stop escaping your pain through a bottle of alcohol. Then, come follow me. Daughter, I want you to stop binge-eating when you're stressed out. Then, come follow me." Insert your own idol here. What is the one thing you can't give up, all the while reading your Bible every morning? All the while going through the motions of life. All the while leading Bible study or, like me, your child's Sunday school class.

Like the rich young ruler, I had been following all the rules, yet completely missing the abundant Christian life. I had been bowing down to idols that don't give two cents about me. And for the longest time, I didn't even realize it—until the week I taught a Sunday school class of five- and six-year-olds about the rich young ruler. It took sweet first graders to wake me up. In the lesson that day, the children were asked to think about something they owned that meant more to them than it should, something perhaps that had become more important in their lives than Jesus. It's hard explaining what an idol is to a young child, but one by one, they named their most precious possessions: an LOL doll, an iPad, a collection of figures. One little boy reluctantly laid down his Pokémon cards on the table and said that it was hard to buy the best cards since he only gets five dollars in allowance a week. Another sweet girl came to me with tears in her big blue eyes and said that she thinks that she may love her puppy more than Jesus. Another kid ran to her purse and handed me her makeup kit. Do you see? These sweet first graders got it! And the longer I watched their reluctance become surrender, the more I got it. No, I did more than get it. The innocence of these children's honest confessions hit me like a Mack truck. You see, I may not love a particular item like these kids do, but I sure as heck bow down to the god of comfort, the god of pleasure, the god of approval—and then there's the god named Kim. And she makes a terrible god.

Remember that season I mentioned earlier where I told you my marriage sucked? It's hard to believe now, but for *years*, I literally could not stand the man next to me. *He* was wrapped up in work. *He* was not romantic. *He* was selfish. And *he* definitely was not in tune with *my* needs. (I was perfect, of course.) Seriously, between my expectations and his hyper focus on work and his buddies, we had a long, bad season. During these years, I leaned into Jesus. I bathed in his word. I prayed and fasted for my man.

I'm totally kidding. I was awful. I cried. I said mean things. I manipulated him, and worst of all, I did something stupid and detrimental. I compared my spouse to other men. Men I knew. Men I didn't know. I also watched the mess out of romantic comedies and dramas. Y'all, when your marriage is low, don't watch this garbage. Don't watch *This Is Us* and expect your man to measure up to Jack Pearson. First of all, no one like him exists. Second, no one like him exists. He's a character. A puppet, if you will. It's not good for you to get lost in a dream world of characters living by a script that makes your man look bad. In 1 Corinthians 10 Paul lays it out:

> You say, "I am allowed to do anything"—but not everything is good for you. You say, "I am allowed to do anything"—but not everything is beneficial.
>
> 1 Corinthians 10:23 (NLT)

I wasn't cheating on my spouse. I wasn't watching porn. I was watching a very popular television show that's fairly clean. And if someone were to walk through my front door, the fact that I was watching *This Is Us* wouldn't turn any heads. But in my heart, I would know. I would know that what I was exposing myself to each week was driving a wedge between Andrew and me. I would know that Satan was whispering words into my already fragile soul. I would know that anything that points out all the things that Andrew was *not* is sin. For me, watching shows like *This Is Us* and making unfair comparisons to my husband was a sin. A personal sin. *Personal* sins are no joke. They're actually downright scary, because they are so personal that unless you speak up, they usually go unnoticed. And there's no accountability if there's no exposure. Sisters, we have to acknowledge our personal sins. Those things you crave more than Jesus. That seemingly harmless thing you do for comfort. Give it up. Give up that one thing and follow him. Because these thoughts, these sneaky thoughts, they can lead you down the same path as the rich young ruler. Sell your possessions and follow Jesus.

I don't know about you, but the Covid quarantine in 2020 had me on the struggle bus. It had me eating garbage that absolutely did not fuel my body. I'm talking pasta most nights, dessert, sometimes two dinners. It also had me drinking more than normal, most nights having two glasses of wine. Some of you may be rolling your eyes and thinking, "That's cute. Two glasses." Others may not touch the stuff, but don't miss my point here. If you are doing something with wrong motives, does it matter what it is? In no way am I throwing my conviction on you, by the way. Like I said, sin is very personal, and my unrestrained indulgence with food and wine during that time was wrecking my peace.

After ignoring that conviction for some time, I ultimately made changes for that season. Have I given up wine altogether? Heck no. I love wine. And I firmly believe that wine is like food, meant to be had in fellowship. I actually believe that it can bring glory to Jesus if used in the right way. There's nothing I love more than sitting around a fire with girlfriends, a glass of pinot, and some good conversation. But for that particular season, Jesus wanted me to make changes. It was hard to recognize this. It was even harder to do something about it, because I rationalized that I wasn't getting drunk, but my pleasure needed to be reined in. Sister, what pleasure of yours needs to be reined in? Do you need to take a social media break? Do you need to stop drinking wine? Do you need to refrain from certain TV shows? Do you need to stop shopping for a while? What pleasure has become sin in your life? What technically "lawful" thing has become unprofitable to your well-being or your witness or your walk with Jesus, as Paul warned against? Furthermore, what will you do about it? Charles Spurgeon, one of the most influential and respected preachers in history, minced no words when he preached on that question on October 12, 1876:

> *Then, in the strength of that name, go up and kill your bosom sin and your constitutional sin—and never rest till you have driven your dagger through every evil that lurks within your soul!*[1]

Thank you, Charles Spurgeon. Just thank you.

We live in an era where you can literally find acceptance for just about anything. Sadly, this means that if you don't want to change, you don't have to. You can skate through life without giving anything up, especially that sin that's so easy to hide. But if you love Jesus, I mean truly love Jesus, you will lack peace until you give it up—and lacking peace is no way to live. Why? Because the Lord didn't die for you to merely "exist." Jesus himself said in John 10:10, *"The thief comes only to steal and kill and destroy. I came that they may have life and have it abundantly"* (ESV). So, I ask you: What area is the thief stealing abundant life from you? What evil lurks within your soul? Whatever it is, it's not worth it. Pornography. Alcohol. Food. TV choices. Social media. Promiscuity. Materialism. Whatever is wrecking your peace, nail it to the cross.

Sisters, we have to acknowledge our personal sins. Those things you crave more than Jesus. That seemingly harmless thing you do for comfort. Give it up. Give up that one thing and follow him.

There's an incredible story in Genesis 25 that captures our culture perfectly. It's the story of Jacob and Esau. Jacob and Esau were twins. Esau was born first, likely by just a few minutes, but birth order was a huge deal back in the day. The firstborn was the heir to everything. Jacob was born literally holding Esau's heel, foreshadowing the fact that he would get ahead of his brother in line. Fast forward a little and Jacob

---

[1] Charles H. Spurgeon, Sermon #2864, October 12, 1876, Metropolitan Tabernacle, London.

has become a mama's boy and, well, a little bratty. Esau, in turn, becomes quite the outdoorsman. One day Esau comes in from spending some time in the open country and smells something fantastic in the kitchen. He is so hungry that he tells his brother Jacob to give him some of that yummy soup. Jacob, seeking an opportunity to manipulate the situation, tells Esau that he can have all the soup he wants if he will give him his birthright, aka the blessing of the firstborn. Naturally, Esau is only thinking of his immediate needs and is, like, "Sure, dude, whatever." And just like that, Jacob receives Esau's birthright. I used to read this story as a kid and had no idea the gravity of it, but I get it now. This exchange literally changes the entire dynamic of both their lives forever. Esau is now number two in terms of rank. He is no longer the next in line all because of his need for instant gratification.

You may look at this story and think Esau is an absolute idiot. I know I do, but we need to cut Esau a little slack. Truth is, we all have the potential to do what he did. Actually, I'll take that further. We have all sold ourselves for instant gratification a time or two—or five hundred. Binge-eating after months of changing our lifestyle. Saying something hateful in the heat of the moment. Getting drunk instead of dealing with our feelings. Spending money to feel validated. Pick your poison. And here's the scary thing. If we don't reign this in, we could easily trade our callings for some pleasure that's just not worth it. Some small thing that is seemingly innocent, like looking at our ex's life on social media or drinking a glass or two every night or cutting corners at work. Before you know it, you've sold your birthright for something destructive, something that can numb your life just enough to suppress Jesus. So, I'm going to ask you this again: What are you trading?

I have this one sin I've dealt with my whole life. A sin that feeds into other sins. A stronghold if you will. I can think back to when I was a young adolescent and I struggled with it. I hate this sin. I abhor it. It has taken so much from me. I've made some progress, but when things are rough or when I'm not in the Word, it's the first thing I run to, like a moth to the flame. Did I mention that I hate it? And the crazy thing, the scary thing is that most people that know me probably don't even know about this problem of mine. But it's just that. A problem. And if unchecked, it has the potential to destroy me. It has roughed me up so much in the past. You want to know the sick thing about it? In my weakest moments, it feels good to return to it. Like an old friend, there it is, waiting for me. There's this brief comfort that comes with it, but it doesn't sustain. I always wake up with regret. And I know that I know that I know that it's not supposed to feel this way.

I have struggled with an eating disorder most of my life. Even now. Even as I write this. I have come so far, but it's still there in the distance waiting for me to call out to it. When life is out of control, I turn to food. My self-worth also has a tendency to be wrapped up in how fat or thin I feel. My sense of accomplishment is wrapped up in how well I'm managing this. Listen, I know and you know this is absolute garbage, but that's the thing about sin. We are all one step away from complete destruction. I've had seasons when I was so thin my face looked like a skeleton. I obsessed. I counted calories. I went to bed hungry. I drank coffee and Diet Coke to suppress my appetite. I was rail thin yet saw a fat girl in the mirror. No size or number was good enough. I have also had seasons where I was fat. I would barely leave my house for fear that people would see how fat I was. How weak I was for letting myself get this way. I ate my feelings. I couldn't fit in my clothes. I ignored mirrors for fear of what I saw.

You see, this small sin of control over food isn't so small. If unchecked, it sends me in a downward spiral that becomes a full-blown self-esteem problem. It silences me. It has me turning inward. It isolates me. It has me mean. It literally paralyzes me. For me this has been a lifelong struggle and probably always will be. It's a struggle that I fight with everything I have because I am more motivated than ever to nail it to the cross. You see, I have a baby girl who watches me. I also have two sons who look to me to model what a wife and mother looks like. All I have to say is, Satan better watch out, because you better believe I will do everything in my power not to show my children a defeated mother. They may see my flaws, but they will also see a determined mother with her face in the Word. A mother who fights her sin on her knees and who finds her worth in the Lord, not on the scale. I have finally named this sin for what it is and while it does flare up from time to time, I know how to fight it. But make no mistake. Satan wants to use it to destroy me. What secret sin does he want to use to destroy you?

What secret sin has you? What do you hide, big or small, that effects your entire well-being? Is it a shopping addiction? An eating disorder?

Do you look at other people's husbands? Do you drink in secret? Whatever it is, name it. Name it and deal with it. Be aware of it lurking in the alley. Know that when you are weak you will want to return to it. But guess what? Just because you want to return to it doesn't mean it has to engulf you. You can have victory over it. God wants to infuse his strength in you to have victory over it. Listen up and listen hard: God did not send his baby boy to the cross for us to run around a hamster wheel with habitual sin. He wants us victorious. He has given us everything we need to be victorious. So be a victor not a victim.

Anyone else have a sin like mine? A personal sin you reason doesn't hurt anyone? It could be your choice of television. You may watch something innocent like *Fixer Upper* or *House Hunters* but deep down you know it's not healthy. You know that you struggle with envy. Envy that turns to criticism. Bitterness. Inadequacy in your work or your husband's ability to provide. Cut it off. Or maybe you're a binge-eater. You run to food when things are bad. You eat to the point of lethargy. You won't leave the house because you feel so fat. Cut it off. Or maybe there's a guy at work you flirt with. You're married so you would never do anything crazy, but the emails. The little conversations. They give you butterflies. Cut it off. Or maybe it's porn. Or shopping. Or alcohol. I'll say it again. Cut it off. Even if it's a secret sin no one knows about. Even if you tell yourself it's innocent. Sister, nothing is innocent if it wrecks your peace. That nagging feeling you have after you partake in this sin, it's called conviction. If unchecked this sin may soon defeat you; and you and I were not made to live in defeat.

Now, before you say that you've come to terms with this sin, before you accept it as just a part of who you are, let me remind you that this is not God's best for you. It is not a part of you that you should just accept. In fact, there's no room in your life for it. You may be able to stop cold turkey. You may need some accountability. You may need counseling. Your sin may be a full-blown addiction that needs intensive intervention. This is why you have to share your secret sin with someone. You need accountability. You need help. We all do. Because like I said, we weren't created for defeat. Of course relapses happen. Of course we have the tendency to return to old habits. We are human, but the difference now is that you recognize that sin. You put a name on it. You have told someone about it. You have accepted that it's paid for. You may have to nail it to the cross daily—I know I do. The difference now is that you have accepted that Jesus died for it. No matter what it is, he died for it. No matter what it is, Satan doesn't get to tell you that your worth is tied up in it. Now get excited because the spiral you have been traveling is now a straight line—and that line is the path to freedom in Jesus.

And if your right hand causes you to sin, cut it off and throw it away. For it is better that you lose one of your members than that your whole body go into hell.

Matthew 5:30 (ESV)

6

Sister, stand up.

*Listening to gossip is like
eating cheap candy;
do you really want junk like
that in your belly?*
Proverbs 18:8 (MSG)

GOSSIP. THERE, I admit it. I say things about people all the time that I shouldn't. I usually rationalize it by saying things like, "I would say it to their face," but truth is I wouldn't. Sometimes I'll tell people I'm just "venting." And there's the classic prayer request rationalization. I used to tell myself that what I do isn't that bad. I mean, I don't say things about people that are untrue. I'm nothing like that coworker of mine who gets all hushed and tells you things that you shouldn't know. But here's the God's honest truth: I listen. Truth is, I want to know. I love to hear things I shouldn't. And do you want to know why? Because it makes me feel important. What an insecure, horrible thought, but I'm admitting it because I want you to admit it too. When that toxic coworker of mine tells me all the things, not only do I listen, but I go back for more. When I say I gossip, I say that as in this is still a struggle for me. And even though I don't chime in, listening is still gossip.

I'd like to say the Holy Spirit gently reminded me about this in my quiet time one morning, but that's a lie. I actually learned this in the hardest of ways. I learned this when I was the one being talked about, when my confidant, my coworker, and my friend turned around and gossiped about me to my coworkers and to my boss. And if that wasn't bad enough, they actually believed her. It hurt. A lot. It created an atmosphere of insecurity in a place that once felt like home. I was unable to make eye contact with people I once called friends. Ultimately, gossip pushed me to quit a job I loved. The thing is, had I not listened, had I not been a part of the gossip, it may have stopped with me. Sister, gossip isn't gossip if you shut it down. And I failed to do that. Learn from my mistake.

At best, gossip is toxic. But, in reality, spreading damaging rumors about another person is like murdering them with words. Y'all, gossip is not an "acceptable" sin to just glaze over, and as someone who has been on the receiving end, it's infuriating! It renders you helpless, because there's nothing you can do but take it. You can try to defend yourself, but here's the thing about toxic people. They don't listen. And they certainly don't stop spraying their poison just because you're sad. Truth is, they don't give a cent about you or your feelings. You see, toxic people are not safe. They cannot be reasoned with. They dance over the satisfaction of hurting others, so confronting people like this is like throwing gasoline on a flame. But I tried anyway. I was so insecure, I had to cover my bases. I went to the listeners to make sure they knew that I was amazing and awesome and, oh, so godly. Please, for the love of mankind, don't do this. Not only is this unnecessary, but it gets old fast. I was exhausted. I cried a lot. In my car. To my mom. To Andrew. Once even to the checkout lady at Target. I was mean to my family. Basically I was miserable. But this experience needed to happen so I would learn. I needed to get to the root of why I began listening to this garbage in the first place. I needed to examine the core of why I liked hearing idle gossip myself.

Let me ask you some of the same questions I asked myself when I did some deep reflecting. Why do you gossip? And when I say gossip, I don't mean spreading malicious lies. That could be part of it, but that's not true for most of us gossipers. Most of us just chit chat. We process out loud about others' lives, usually over lunch or a glass of wine. And the crazy thing is that we don't realize we're doing it. So again, I ask you, why do you gossip? Do you need to feel important by being in the know? Do you need to feel included? Do you like to see others fall? Are you bored?

Are you avoiding something in your own life? Do you see something in someone that you're scared you will become? Why do we salivate when we hear that some perfect person is far from it?

As I reflected on this question, I realized that my main reason for gossiping is to feel important. I'm a very relational person. I want to bond with people so badly that I want to give them something hot off the press. I want to have the satisfaction of being there to tell someone something I know and they don't. Pathetic, I know, but I promised you transparency, so here it is. Bonding over someone else's brokenness is not the way to bond. Telling someone your opinion about another person's misery is not a way to strengthen a friendship. Spreading private or unconfirmed information, whether through prayer, concern, or straight-up malice, is wrong. True or not, it's not your story to tell. And my word, just go to a spin class or have a cup of coffee if you want to bond with someone so badly.

Maybe you're different than me. Maybe you gossip because you're insecure. Maybe you feel a need to elevate yourself by putting someone else down. Maybe a subtle one-up on some seemingly "perfect" girl makes you feel a little better about yourself. I get it. I promise I get it. I actually own the T-shirt on this subject. But it's still wrong. It's dead wrong and not the way of Christ. Jesus was perfect and had every reason to brag, yet he never did. In fact, he was so secure in who he was that he postured himself beneath others. If we could only be that secure in our calling. Ephesians 4:29 says:

> *Let no corrupting talk come out of your mouths, but only such as is good for building up, as fits the occasion, that it may give grace to those who hear.*
>
> Ephesians 4:29 (ESV)

Is everything you say good for building people up? Do your words give grace to those who hear them? Because when you leave a conversation, you shouldn't question if it's right or wrong. You shouldn't feel icky. You shouldn't have to call and apologize after you've processed what just went down. In fact, you should speak in such a way that others feel better after having been with you. And stronger. And a little more in love with Jesus.

A good person produces good things from the treasury of a good heart, and an evil person produces evil things from the treasury of an evil heart. What you say flows from what is in your heart.

Luke 6:45 (NLT)

I have a friend named Hillary. She's amazing. Everyone needs a friend like her. She's the kind of friend who sees the good in everyone. You know this kind of friend. Maybe you're this kind of friend. The kind of friend that can find that one tiny speck of good in anyone or any situation. That friend who gives everyone the benefit of the doubt. The friend who speaks words of kindness about everyone, present or not. My friend Hillary could catch wind of a high-profile scandal and never utter a word to a soul. She could be in a group of women talking negatively about someone she barely knows, and my Hilly is going to speak something kind to the group. Why? Because she truly understands the power of her words. Friends like her infect me in the best of ways. Surrounding myself with people like her make me better. They hold me accountable because, you better believe, friends like her aren't going to let me fall into the insecure habit of trying to be important by way of gossip. Friends like her don't have to whisper. These are the kind of people we should surround ourselves with. These are the kind of women we should be charging life with. These are the kind of women who will build you up when you aren't in the room. These are the kind of women we should all strive to be.

Hear me loud and clear when I say this: it's not enough to simply not gossip about someone or to not listen to gossip. I'll say it another way. Simply remaining silent when your friend, church member, or coworker is being gossiped about isn't enough. It's the sissy way out. I don't care if this high road leaves you eating alone in the break room, this is the way of the Cross. This is the *only* way and should be your *only* response. We aren't in middle school anymore. Walking away is not good enough for godly adults. When I was in the thick of being gossiped about, I would have given anything for someone to have had my back, for some confident person to have pointed out the fact that I'm a Jesus-loving woman who is rooted in good intentions. I didn't have this. Most of us don't have this, but what is it they say? Be the kind of friend you want to be. Be the kind of woman you want in your life. Be a Hillary.

Simply remaining silent when your friend, church member, or coworker is being gossiped about isn't enough. It's the sissy way out. I don't care if this high road leaves you eating alone in the break room, this is the way of the Cross. This is the only way and should be your only response.

———————

Sisters, we have no need to compete with one another. There's plenty of seats at the table. We have no need to be jealous or insecure of each other. We all have our own unique calling. What is God's unique instruction to you? Do you really have to be the best at everything at the expense of tearing someone down? Do you really have to one-up a sister who is serving where God has called her simply because you have the sick need to compete? We have a God who has told us our worth. A God who loves us no matter what people say. A God who loves us no matter how nasty our hearts. Repeat after me. You are seen. You are loved. You are beautiful. You are worthy.

This all sounds lovely on paper, but I hear your question. What on earth does this even look like? How do you start over after everything you've already said and done and just stop talking badly about people? It's actually quite easy. You confess with your mouth and then you repent in your heart. Simply tell Jesus you know you do this. Tell him you are aware that this is a problem, then you stop. Just like that. You may need to repair the damage you've caused. You may need to apologize to some folks. You may have to shrink your circle for a bit. But you can end this charade just like that. You know what also helps? Finding your calling. I promise you. Scout's honor, I promise you, that once you find your calling, you will be so wrapped up in your mission for Jesus that what your coworker says about someone else or even you won't even be on your radar. You will be so lost in Jesus that you won't even think twice about what someone else is doing or saying.

Make a careful exploration of who you are and the work you have been given, and then sink yourself into that. Don't be impressed with yourself. Don't compare yourself with others. Each of you must take responsibility for doing the creative best you can with your own life.

Galatians 6:4–5 (MSG)

Simply not gossiping about people is for kids. That's what we teach our babies. You're a grown-up. You're a godly, confident adult at that. Stand up for people. Find the good in everyone. Cheer others on. We need you. I need you.

Therefore encourage one another and build one another up.

1 Thessalonians 5:11a (ESV)

7

Sister, are you angry?

A fool is quick-tempered,
but a wise person stays calm
when insulted.

Proverbs 12:16 (NLT)

I'VE ALWAYS JUSTIFIED my anger, and I'm not talking mad-at-my-husband angry. I mean mad at the way people are treated or angry at the way the poor are neglected. Y'all, my super-charged sense of righteous indignation rattles me to the core. It wakes me up at night. It makes me want to throw things at people. For real, I feel a sense of rage when I see people being exploited—animals, babies, the elderly. I can't handle it. And while I believe that this sensitivity to the innocent is justified, I'm pretty sure my reactions are not.

I think we all get worked up on different levels about various things. Some of us aren't as expressive as others, but almost all of us feel a sense of injustice in some capacity. You can't live in our world and not feel something. Shoot, just scroll on social media or turn on the news. But I'm not talking about the *feeling* of injustice here. That part is a spiritual reaction, a sensitivity in line with the gospel. If you know anything about Jesus, you know that he is protective of the poor, both monetarily and in spirit. He has a soft heart for the broken. The underserved. The nobodies. The underdog. So, do not think by any means I am saying that feeling the need to speak for those who can't speak for themselves is even remotely wrong. On the contrary. Proverbs 31 actually commands us to do so:

Speak up for those who cannot speak for themselves; ensure justice for those being crushed. Yes, speak up for the poor and helpless, and see that they get justice.

Proverbs 31:8-9 (NLT)

There is no disputing our obligation to speak for those who have no voice, but it's more than that. I'm talking about the manner in which we express ourselves. I would guess that nine out of ten times we are not in line with *how* God wants us respond.

You may know the story about Jesus turning over the tables in the New Testament. If not, it's found in all four Gospels (Matthew 21:12–13; Mark 11:15–18; Luke 19:45–46; John 2:13–17). Here's what happened. Jesus went to the temple—"my house," he called it—during the beginning of Passover. This is the time when the temple and basically all of Jerusalem would have been filled with people from all over, coming to pay their temple tax and bring their animal sacrifices. When Jesus went to the temple, he saw activities happening among the money changers and sellers that was so sinful and irreverent to his Father that he was filled with righteous indignation. He was mad, I mean mad, at the fact that people brought their sin into his house as if it were no big deal. So, how did he respond? He turned the tables over and exposed these people. He even chased them out of the temple. Jesus was angry and he expressed it. But notice I said he was filled with righteous indignation. Stay with me here.

For years, I have given myself a pass on my own expression of anger with this story in mind. Over and over again, I have convinced myself that I have permission from Jesus for my emotional outbursts when, in fact, most of the triggers for my anger have nothing to do with "righteous indignation." I'd even say that just about every time I overreact, my outburst is due to my own lack of self-control—of feeling sinned against or wanting justice.

I'm a highly emotional person. I'm reactive. Maybe too reactive. I feel everything deeply and intensely. One thing I've learned is that feelings can't be trusted. They invade like cancer and can easily take over reason. As I get older, I'm learning that feelings don't always need to be expressed out loud. Some of them should be, for sure, but more often than not, time and prayer chill those suckers out. Maybe you're nothing like me. Maybe you possess more self-control. Maybe you don't feel things much at all. Or maybe, just maybe, you suppress your emotions, burying them so deep that it affects your health. Maybe you express your emotions through unhealthy habits such as binge-eating, shopping, excessive drinking, or overexercising. Maybe you can't deal with big feelings, so you channel them into something else. Maybe you choose to hit the ignore button. You get lost in a Netflix binge, park it in yoga pants, and worship the god of comfort. Personally, I have always justified reacting in the moment. It's action-oriented. It's an attention-getter. It definitely drives a point home. And after all, isn't that what Jesus did in the temple? Kinda. Not really. No. Not at all.

Jesus is an enigma. You can't limit him to a certain personality. Apart from the fact that he always has God's glory in mind, he is unpredictable. He is peace and passion all in one. He is like the strong, healthy form of every personality. This is precisely why I've always used the temple cleansing story to justify my reaction to injustice. Jesus is perfect yet he turned over tables. He chased people out of the temple, for crying out loud. Surely, I mean surely, this means I get a pass to react the way I see fit to the things I find unjust, right?

I have some bad news. The story about Jesus turning tables over is an exception, not his usual reaction, and not even in the same ballpark as the table-turning reactions I have. Don't get me wrong. His anger was 100 percent justified. Unfortunately, we can't use this example to validate every emotional outburst. In fact, there are significantly more verses throughout Scripture about *not* reacting. My favorite is in Romans 12:

> *Don't insist on getting even; that's not for you to do. "I'll do the judging," says God. "I'll take care of it."*
>
> Romans 12:19b (MSG)

Want to know my problem with this verse? Everything. Seriously, do you want to know why I get so worked up about people? I think, deep down, I don't trust God to punish those who wrong me or those I love. I don't trust him to put hypocritical, demeaning jerks in their place. And by the majority of what I read on social media, I'm not sure a lot of

Christians do either. If you're constantly slamming people with your harsh rhetoric, then, like me, you're taking matters into your own hands. I don't care if you're right or they deserve it, if you react harshly to every injustice, you need to get to the root of why. Because here's the deal, no matter how justified, insults have never led anyone to the Cross. They may make you feel better for a few minutes, but ultimately they lead people away from Jesus all together.

Let me ask you a question. If you middle-finger someone for speaking poorly about your kid, what does this accomplish? Sure it feels good to give some scumbag a piece of your mind, but long term, how does this reaction reflect the heart of Jesus? Moreover, how does it evoke change? I get the fact that you may be standing up for someone or something, but at what cost? If your ultimate intention is to share the gospel, then you've failed. Let me interject here and say that I write this with the heaviest of hearts. For real, I feel like a big, fat hypocrite because this is my biggest struggle, so big that it would be far easier not to write about it. But God reminded me that the fact that this is my biggest struggle means that I should absolutely be writing about it. The struggle is real, and of course I say all these things because I have a story.

I have a coworker who hates me. At least it feels like she hates me. All the signs are there. She won't look me in the eye. Ever. She sighs loudly whenever I speak. She even talks about me in the third person when I'm sitting right there. Then there's the time she yelled at me. Like I said, all the signs are there. In a recent meeting, she said something about a patient that was so stinking mean that I almost came out of my seat. Instead of taking a breath and seeing just how lost and lonely this woman is, I resorted to lashing out. Instead of showing her Jesus, I decided to put her in her place. Actually, there was no deciding—only reacting. I was condescending. I deliberately made her look like an absolute idiot. I exposed her mean heart, yet in doing that I helped no one. In fact, everyone lost here. I acted in no way, shape, or form like Jesus, and guess what? This person left our meeting feeling no more compassion for our patient than when she walked in, and she even had more fuel to feed her negative feelings toward me. Because of my need to put her in her place, this woman could not see Jesus. Let's be real here. When has an angry response of any kind ever reached someone's heart in a transformational way? When has an insult or one-up ever softened anyone? It hasn't. It may shut someone up for the moment, but it doesn't represent Jesus. No matter how reprehensible the situation is, Christians have no reason to sin in their response to evil. Never. Ever. Ever.

> *Don't sin by letting anger control you. Think about it overnight and remain silent.*
>
> Psalm 4:4 (NLT)

As much as I want to ignore this verse, I can't. And for someone with a confrontational personality and a hot temper this is excruciatingly painful. I can't stand to see injustice of any kind. I used to think that made me an awesome person. I used to think I was God's special little soldier given a mission to fight every injustice, but the roots of my encounters are usually far from godly. In fact, they are usually rooted in pride and unbelief. Pride because thinking that God has to use me to fight his fights is extremely arrogant. Unbelief in my sheer doubt that God will take care of it. I'm not saying this means we should tolerate injustice. Not in the least. But we should not be sinning in our response to it. In fact, the question we should all be asking ourselves is this: Are we trying to be "right" or are we trying to be holy? Are we mad that someone is sinning against us or are we mad that they are sinning against God? Because when I mouthed off to my coworker in that meeting, part of it was because she treated my patient poorly. But another part, the bigger part, was because she had been treating *me* poorly.

> ### No matter how reprehensible the situation is, Christians have no reason to sin in their response. Never. Ever. Ever.

We will never win people to Jesus like this. My coworker will never know of God's love if I treat her with contempt. And she's miserable. She needs to see something different. She needs to see compassion—to be *shown* compassion. She needs to see grace. She needs to see someone who represents Jesus. One-upping her in a public arena did one thing and one thing only. It repelled Jesus. And I may never have the chance to correct that. Shame on me and my quick need for satisfaction.

Here's the thing. There's anger—and there's righteous anger. Anger is being mad. In the case with my mean-girl coworker, I was angry. And in my state of anger, I was concerned about myself. *My* feelings. *My* need to give her what I thought she deserved. But righteous anger? Y'all, righteous anger has only one concern, and that's Jesus. When expressing it as Jesus did in the temple and throughout Scripture, there was never sin involved. There was no gossip. Jesus didn't go to his disciples and loop them in on the issue. He didn't find the need to defend his every move. He simply pointed folks to his father. Without slander. Without posting it on social media. Without cursing or middle-fingering. Righteous anger is intentional. It doesn't make reactive, irrational decisions. It doesn't mouth off. It doesn't one-up. It's controlled. It's calculated. It's directed at sin, not toward someone's character.

In Mark 3, Jesus models self-control so perfectly when he healed a man on the Sabbath. For those of you who don't get the full meaning of this, let me assure you that this was a huge faux pas. Doing work on the Sabbath was the cardinal sin in those days. Naturally, the Pharisees were livid. They were all about the rules. They couldn't wrap their tiny heads around the importance of grace and law. Jesus had every reason to one-up. He had every reason to put these hypocrites in their place, but he didn't. According to Mark 3:5, Jesus looked around at the Pharisees in anger, "deeply distressed at their stubborn hearts," and healed the man anyway. He didn't flip them off. He didn't throw anything. He didn't say, "Booyah!" He remained confident in his purpose and completed the task in front of him. Was he mad? Heck, yeah, he was, but he channeled his anger by keeping on with his purpose. Pointing people to the Father was Jesus' MO. It should be ours as well.

Jesus is our litmus test. He is the bar in which we should measure our reactions against. Our social media fights. Our one-upping. Our attempt to fight the war of injustice with words and action. Y'all, it's all fruitless and certainly not the way of Jesus. It may feel good to unload for a minute, but those words serve no purpose. Can you imagine if we rewired our anger and used that same intensity to pray for the injustices of this world? Can you imagine if we rerouted all that rage toward love? Can you imagine if we could throw all those emotions toward heaven? Can you imagine if we used all that energy toward pleading for souls? Can you imagine the crowd we would have in heaven?

Understand this, my dear brothers and sisters: You must all be quick to listen, slow to speak, and slow to get angry. Human anger does not produce the righteousness God desires.

James 1:19–20 (NLT)

8

Sister, just say yes!

You know that look women get when they
want to have sex? Me neither.
Steve Martin

SOMETIMES I USE my kids as sex blockers. Rarely but sometimes. Okay, often. But only if I'm really tired. And before you judge me, everyone does this to some extent. Most of my friends pretend to be asleep. Or pick a fight. Some just say no and roll over. At least my excuse is family-oriented. Seriously, I don't care who you are, everyone has some tactic they use in attempts to repel their horny husband. But it's not because we don't love them. We're just tired. So tired. For lots of reasons. Some of us work. Some of us have had kids hanging on us all day. Some of us have bitterness toward our spouse. Some of us hate the way we look. Sadly, all of these reasons are killjoys to a hoppin' sex life. And, if you're married, then you should be having a fantastic sex life—or be working toward one. Because here's the truth. Sex shouldn't suck. It shouldn't be a dreaded chore. It shouldn't be vanilla. And it shouldn't cause fights. It was created by God for married people to connect souls. Sisters, sex is a gift! It should be had often and it should be good! Please don't write me off here. I'm not a blindly subservient wife who doesn't get the struggle. The struggle is real. So real, in fact, that I have to address this issue head-on, because good sex is vital to a healthy marriage.

Whether you are tired or not, an unfulfilling sex life is a real problem for lots of reasons, but let's start with how men are wired. I don't have man parts, but I've been told that men deal with lust in ways I will never understand. With the increasing rate of reported pornography and infidelity, I believe this. Before I continue, let me be clear. I am in no way saying that it's a woman's fault if her husband cheats or vice versa. *Do not hear that.* Nor am I saying that it's the spouse's fault if a man or woman has a sex or pornography addiction. This chapter is not for you if you fall into any of these categories. I am, however, speaking specifically to tired married women like myself. So if this is you, hear me loud and clear when I say this next part: stop denying your husband what he craves most in life: sex! And not just get-it-over-with sex. I am talking about off-the-charts, good, orgasmic, God-ordained sex—the kind God had in mind when he created it.

Did you catch what I just wrote? God created sex. For our pleasure, yes, but also for our spouse. I'm not gonna lie, sometimes you just do it, even if you're tired. First Corinthians 13 tells us that love is not self-seeking. As in it's not about you. So, yes, sometimes you do it when you're tired because you love your man and he wants sex. Welcome to Christian marriage. But remember what I said earlier? I said sex should be good, not just taking one for the team. I don't know about you, but I don't want to be a robot. I want biblical, God-created sex with the man I pledged to have sex with until death do us part! I want fireworks in the bedroom. I want to act like a newlywed, so to speak. I want to put my kids to bed with the anticipation of a fun evening in the bedroom. And I want that for you too. That's why I'm going to point you to the ultimate example of sex. I'm talking make-you-blush, mind-blowing, "can't wait for the kids to get to bed" kind of sex goals. And guess what? It's in the Bible.

Song of Songs was written by King Solomon, and it is the perfect picture of courtship, marriage, foreplay, and sex. In fact, I get a little red when I read it. Song of Songs chapter 7 is basically foreplay between husband and wife—something I find key to a good sex life.

Shapely and graceful your sandaled feet, and queenly your movement—
Your limbs are lithe and elegant, the work of a master artist.
Your body is a chalice, wine-filled.

*Your skin is silken and tawny like a field of wheat touched by the
  breeze.*
Your breasts are like fawns, twins of a gazelle.
Your neck is carved ivory, curved and slender.
Your eyes are wells of light, deep with mystery.
Quintessentially feminine!
Your profile turns all heads, commanding attention.
The feelings I get when I see the high mountain ranges
—stirrings of desire, longings for the heights—
Remind me of you, and I'm spoiled for anyone else!
*Your beauty, within and without, is absolute, dear lover, close
  companion.*
You are tall and supple, like the palm tree,
and your full breasts are like sweet clusters of dates.
*I say, "I'm going to climb that palm tree! I'm going to caress its
  fruit!"*
Oh yes! Your breasts will be clusters of sweet fruit to me,
*Your breath clean and cool like fresh mint, your tongue and lips like
  the best wine.*
Yes, and yours are, too—my love's kisses flow from his lips to mine.
I am my lover's. I'm all he wants. I'm all the world to him!
Come, dear lover—let's tramp through the countryside.
*Let's sleep at some wayside inn, then rise early and listen to
  bird-song.*
*Let's look for wildflowers in bloom, blackberry bushes blossoming
  white,*
Fruit trees adorned with cascading flowers.
And there I'll give myself to you, my love to your love!

Song of Songs 7:1–12 (MSG)

Is this you? Are you having awesome sex like Solomon and the
Shulamite woman? Are you admiring your husband, dad bod and all?
Is there foreplay? Desire? Anticipation? Or are you checking that box
any time you "allow" your spouse to join you for a quick round of inter-
course? Or worse, are you constantly saying no to a need that feels basic
to most men? If so, then you are setting your man up for failure because,
guess what! You are the only sex your man is getting. You, sister, are

literally holding hostage the one thing your man needs, and no matter the justification, it's not cool. Not cool at all. And the reason I know that it's not cool is because I did it for years.

When Andrew and I first got married, I literally thought I would need to submit FMLA paperwork because we couldn't go a day without having sex multiple times. For a few months it was seriously our hobby. Sadly, the newness wore off. Then we got busy with work. And life. Then we had kids. Kids who started filling so much of my need for touch that frankly my husband's hands on my body were just another person needing something. I mean, who wants to have sex when you've been wiping butts and nursing babies all day? Then there's the fact that I'm not as skinny as I once was, especially after each birth. I remember once looking down at myself post-shower and I screamed. Like I'm not joking. I screamed out loud. At my own body. The saggy skin. My nonexistent boobs. There was a real season in my life where I could have stored things in the cellulite on the back of my thighs. And did I mention the fact that I'm tired? I'm always tired. By the time my kids are asleep, I'm done. There could be an earthquake, and I promise you that I would just lay there peacefully awaiting Jesus. But sure enough, just as my body would fall into that deep relaxation mode and I'm drifting off to my happy place, I would feel my husband's hot breath on my ear. "Want a back rub?" he'd ask. Forgive my candidness, but a man asking for sex when you are half asleep is almost as miserable as being woken up in the middle of the night by a barfing kid. Actually, it's worse. And if you don't know what I'm talking about, then you're either lying to yourself or I need to know what meds your doc is prescribing. That being said, if this is you, if you are holding out for whatever reason, it can get better. I promise it can get better.

> **Stop denying your husband what he craves most in life: sex! And not just get-it-over-with sex. I am talking about off-the-charts, good, orgasmic, God-ordained sex—the kind God had in mind when he created it.**

For a few years, I found it easier to just fake it because the fights about not getting enough action were more draining then the act of sex itself. Anyone with me here? Anyone else pretending when they would have rather been running in the heat or standing in line at the post office? Sadly, your husband knows how you're feeling. He may be a dunce when it comes to anniversary gifts or putting the kids to bed on time, but I promise you that your husband knows you are avoiding sex. He knows. Mine knew. While I thought I could win an Oscar for my bedroom performance, Andrew knew I didn't want to be there. And all jokes aside, I knew the brokenness in that. I knew that this wasn't the way life should be. I knew that sex was a gift, that my husband seeing past my large backside and still wanting me was pretty incredible. And did I mention that sex is supposed to be awesome? I mean, turn on the TV. It's all the rage. Sex sells, yet here I was, telling my husband it's "that time of the month" for the third week in a row to escape being with him. Y'all, this was all kinds of messed up. I was in my young thirties. I had a lifetime to look forward to with Andrew. I was not about to spend the next fifty years dodging sex. There had to be a change, and after a few years of this cycle, I *wanted* there to be a change.

While it feels really awkward asking God to make you horny, the thought of spending the rest of my marriage avoiding sex seemed worse. Besides, I'm no faker. It's just not who I am. Go big or go home has always been my motto, so I decided to get help. I did what any Christian woman should do when dealing with something difficult—I went to one of my spiritual mentors to talk about it. After all, this sweet lady had a couple of decades on me. For years she has encouraged me in my spiritual life. Surely, she would have some wisdom to impart about this whole sex issue. Seeing as she has always been open about her marriage, I flat out asked her one day. Between sips of iced tea on her screen porch, I began throwing out some pretty direct questions. First, I asked her how often I should have sex with my husband.

Her answer was, "Yes."

Huh? That's not a number. Then I asked her what to do if I was really tired.

"Yes," she said again.

Lastly, I asked her what to do if I wasn't interested at all.

"Yes," she said again and went on to explain.

My sweet, honest mentor shared with me what she had learned through her many years of marriage and about her husband's perspective on the subject. She told me that having sex with your man sets him up for success. She also told me that many men have this deep-rooted fear that they can't please their wives in the bedroom and that lying there all dead fish is detrimental to their soul. After some deep talks with her husband, she learned that, when she has sex with him, he feels like a king. All day. He's more productive at work, more helpful around the house, more affirming. She even once saw him dancing while he was mowing the lawn after they had an afternoon tryst. Obviously, men and women are wired differently, but I wanted in on this positive cycle. I wanted Andrew that happy. I wanted him to feel like a king. I wanted him to feel the way I feel after a good workout or movie. I wanted him to dance when he mowed the lawn! Most of all, I wanted him to feel the same way I feel when he provides me with the security and love I so crave from him.

But I'm so stinkin' tired. Who is with me here? I work. I clean. I mother. I sometimes workout. I have friends. I have a puppy. Who has time to make love all night long, apart from Faith Hill and Tim McGraw? Actually, the more I think about it the more that sounds like a UTI waiting to happen. Besides, by the time the kids are in bed and I've cleaned the dishes, packed lunches, and changed over the laundry, I'm done for. I mean, don't these men get the hats we women wear? We don't just go to work. We are the heart of the home. We raise kids. We get them to all the places. We get stuff done.

I have only been in this marriage thing for a dozen years, but I've learned something very valuable—something backed up by people married fifty years. Sex is vital to a healthy marriage. And when I say sex, I don't mean duty sex. I mean good sex. And while a clean and orderly home are important, they in no way equal the importance of sex. Seriously, my husband would rather me have enough energy to make sexy time than to come home to a clean home. He would rather eat cereal for dinner if it means I have enough energy to initiate sex. I can't even think about the last time I initiated sex. Have I ever? Have you? You see, your man doesn't care if you have shaved legs or not. He just wants sex. He doesn't care if you have saggy boobs or a little wrinkle around the belly button region. He just wants sex. He doesn't care if you're a tad fluffier post-Christmas or after a girls' weekend. He just wants sex. Repeat after me. He just wants sex! Say it out loud. Your man just wants sex! If I need to vacuum for the tenth time to relax, cool, but my man doesn't care. In fact, he will vacuum if it means I'm in our bedroom getting my game face on. He will do the dishes. Shoot, he will even pack lunches. He just wants sex. And not vanilla sex. Don't be lazy. He wants good, chocolate-covered, sprinkles-with-a-cherry-on-top sex. Like I said, go big or go home.

This new way of thinking, however, did require a little work. A lot of work actually, and some changes on both our parts. That's why my husband and I created something I want to share with the world. It was a game changer to our sex life. Get ready because it will change your life too. I almost feel like I should get it trademarked because it's that amazing. Are you ready? Okay, here it is. The Twenty-four Hour Rule. Before I continue, you're welcome.

Here's how it works. You've had a day from you-know-where. You had to clean the mud off the floor. Again. Your kids missed naps and you had no alone time. You have some serious laundry to put away. Your hubby worked late. Finally, finally, the sun goes down and the kids go to bed. You are about to turn on some Netflix as you devour a pint of ice cream, and sure enough, your dumb butt husband misinterprets your "go away" face as a face that wants sex. He completely misses your body language and, like clockwork, homeboy is all, "Want a back rub?" This, my friends, is where you get to invoke the Twenty-four Hour Rule. I swear, my husband sets his watch the moment it's mentioned. From the moment you utter these three words, you get twenty-four hours to get right with God. To rest. To shave. To listen to Michael Bolton or whatever gets you in the mood. To cut beans from your diet. To pray for the desire to want to have sex. Whatever you need. You get twenty-four hours and then you're up, my friend. And I'm telling you, it works. Call me manipulative, but there's something in this whole sex thing for you too—apart from satisfying sex, which one day you will appreciate.

I'm no psychologist or sex therapist, but I've learned that when your husband's needs are met, when his cup is full, he is a rock star. I mean "Van Halen on crack" rock star. He's in a good mood. He has more energy. He even does the laundry. I once found my husband dancing with the kids in the kitchen to Kidz Bop after I surprised him in the shower one morning. I'm telling you, the results are amazing. And the coolest thing about it is that *you* are much happier too. He's not coming home and playing on his phone. He's engaged. With you. And the kids. And his life. This starts a positive chain reaction and guess what! Sex gets better. It gets good. It's no longer something dreaded or a chore to check off a list. You actually start enjoying it again. And I shudder to say these words, but eventually you will be the initiator. You will turn on Ray LaMontagne. You will trade the grannies for Victoria. There will be foreplay. You will be into it. I promise. From someone who dreaded sex for years and even once resorted to farting in order to repel her husband, I speak truth. You will get excited about sex again. And pretty soon, you will turn on some Paw Patrol for the kids, lock your door, and jump your man's bones in the five minutes you have before someone needs something.

I am my lover's and my lover is mine.

Song of Songs 6:3 (MSG)

9

Sister, you'll be okay again.

For though he wounds, he also bandages.
He strikes, but his hands also heal.

Job 5:18 (NLT)

HAVE YOU EVER hit rock bottom? I'm not talking about when your jeans are so tight you switch to yoga pants or when you yell at your kids because they're fighting for the five hundredth time and you lock yourself in the bathroom. I mean rock bottom as in you want to die. You are so down you can't get any lower. You can't cry because you're out of tears. There's nowhere to run. You can't hide. You think the pain will never end. Have you ever been to that kind of rock bottom? Even if you're not suicidal, you feel hopeless; you don't think you will ever live again, much less smile.

I remember it like it was yesterday. The first sight of blood. The fear. Calling the doctor and telling him there was no movement. Drinking juice and still feeling nothing. Finally, a glimmer of hope. A kick. Little did I know that it was my son's goodbye kick. At least that's what I hoped it was. Because the alternative was worse. The alternative was my son's body swooshing against my womb, lifeless, and I can't bear to believe that. I walked into the doctor's office knowing he was gone but praying I was just being dramatic. My doctor frantically kept listening for a heart-beat, but I told him to stop. Henry was gone.

I had a feeling about this. In fact, just days before I lost Henry, I found myself looking up stillbirths on the Internet. I shuddered as Google led me to pictures of stillborn children being cradled by their grieving mothers. I had fake conversations in my head on what I would say to God if he allowed this to happen to me. Every conversation involved my walking away from him, telling him that no God I followed would do this to a praying mom. In my fear, I bargained. I threatened. I looked up at Jesus and told him out loud that if he ever did that to me, then he would no longer be my God.

Then, it happened.

Have you ever been to this place? Has God ever slayed you like this? Have you ever been in such despair that you can actually relate to the priests in the Bible who would rip their clothes and lament? It's okay to admit it. There's actually freedom in admitting it.

I felt this despair when the doctor told me I had to deliver Henry. It took all I had not to rip my clothes off and fall to the floor, but I did something comparable. I begged the doctor to cut Henry out of me. I screamed through tears as I told him to put me to sleep and take care of it, so I didn't have to feel the weight of everything. He didn't, of course. I sat frozen on the delivery table as it hit me: that night I would hold my baby in my arms for the first and last time. I would hear nothing but silence as his little body left my womb.

When I delivered Henry, my husband was the only one in the room. My mom arrived shortly later. Then my best friend. The texts and emails came pouring in, but no one could give me back what had been taken from me. No one could take away the emotional pain. For once in my life, nothing on this earth could help me. I equate that feeling to screaming loudly in a crowded room and having no one hear you, like a terrible nightmare, only it's your real life.

Prior to losing Henry, I was never in a situation that my mom or dad couldn't fix. I'd never faced something Andrew couldn't handle for me. All my life, I just never had any pain too great to bear. That is, until the day my son died in my womb. That day. That cold December day, medicine failed me. My parents couldn't fix it. Money could not change things. My husband could not fight this battle for me. And worst of all, I couldn't give Henry my life in order to spare his. The only thing I could do was turn to Jesus. The very one I told I would forsake if he did this to me. It's weird. I was angry at him but I clung to him. I knew he took Henry, but I also knew he was holding me. I can't explain this. I can only say that he never let me go. More than that, he never let me let *him* go.

Have you ever been to this place? Pushed against the wall with nowhere to go? I love what Charles Spurgeon said in his 1886 sermon on Job's response to unthinkable loss:

O dear Friend, when your grief presses you to the very dust, worship there![2]

Sister, do you *need* God? I'm not asking if you love him. I'm asking if you have everything you need on this earth already. Because I did. And then, suddenly, I didn't. It's the most helpless, hopeless, scary feeling. But it's precisely why we were created. Please do not feel bad or even condemned if you haven't been to this place yet. You can't really help it if you haven't been pressed to the dust yet. I made it thirty-two years without real pain. You may be fifty and still not there. I have no idea how old Job was, but he, too, had everything—until he didn't.

So, if you love God, if you truly love him, if your heart truly longs to be one with him, it's coming. In some way, shape, or form, it's coming. It may be an illness. It may be a slander. It may be a lonely marriage, but it's coming, and when it does, I want you to remember that you are his no matter what comes your way. You are his child whether you feel it or not. He loves you no matter what you say or feel. If you are in Christ, that doesn't change based on feelings, emotions, or circumstances. You were his before the pain. You are his after the pain. You are his as you kick and scream and rebel during the pain. His presence doesn't leave you in the pain. It doesn't leave you when you are too sad to speak. His presence doesn't change if you don't feel him. Sister, *you are his*!

Before I lost Henry, I had the life I thought I deserved. And here's the messed-up part. I used to think that if everyone would just love Jesus like I did, if everyone would just work hard like I did, if everyone followed the rules like I did, they, too, could have a life like mine. Y'all, everything changed in an instant. Not because I did anything wrong or right. Not because I broke a rule. Just because. And it crushed me. My faith was

---

[2]Tom Carter, comp., *Spurgeon at His Best: Over 2000 Striking Quotations from the World's Most Exhaustive and Widely-Read Sermon Series* (Grand Rapids, MI: Baker Book House, 1988), 240.

shattered. But that's the thing about happiness. It's fleeting. Trying to stay happy will give you emotional whiplash. Your joy can't be tied to happiness. I've been walking with Christ most of my life and I still bought into this. Having heaven on earth was never God's intention for any of us thanks to Adam and Eve. Because of the fall, because humans brought flaws into God's perfect design, there will be pain in this world. Jesus says,

> *I have told you all this so that you may have peace in me. Here on earth you will have many trials and sorrows. But take heart, because I have overcome the world.*

John 16:33 (NLT)

Jesus doesn't say *if* you have trouble. He doesn't say *when* some of you have trouble. He says you *will* have trouble. As in all of us. As in count on it. But look what he says next: *"But take heart, because I have overcome the world."*

I like to picture heaven praying over me the night before I lost Henry. Do you ever think like that? Have you ever imagined angels praying over you? Think to the moment before your diagnosis. Or before you knew of a betrayal. Or the moment just before you lost your job. Or heard the dreaded news. I love to picture Jesus looking down and praying as fervently as he did in the garden. I find great comfort in my belief that heaven was praying as Henry took his last breath in my womb. That Jesus welcomed him in heaven while praying for my broken heart. That Jesus was on his face praying with the same vigor as when he prayed for his own cup to be passed. Only it was his daughter's cup this time. And just as God said no to his boy, he said no to me.

God is sovereign. He knew Henry would die before I was born. He knew the pain of this day when I started my Christian journey in the third grade. He knew I would someday hold my stillborn child every time I lifted my hands in worship. He knew the day before it happened. He was there as Henry took his last breath on earth. I was probably sleeping when Henry died, but God wasn't. He was up all night. When I woke the next morning with a lifeless child in my womb, I had no clue that Jesus was holding Henry in his arms. He was holding my son as I was told, "There's no heartbeat." He was holding Henry as I held his lifeless body. Only, Henry was no longer lifeless. The first face he saw was that of Jesus.

I can't tell you how surreal it is to deliver a baby who makes no sound. It's traumatic. It's unnatural. It is not the way it should be. While losing Henry was the most horrific thing that had ever happened to me, I had to look at the big picture to understand—not those dismissive Christian platitudes about how great heaven is or how God will use it for his glory, but the consistency of God's goodness in my life over the last few decades. I have to remember what Jesus said in John 13 to his disciples when they didn't understand him:

> *Jesus replied, "You don't understand now what I am doing, but someday you will.*
>
> John 13:7 (NLT)

When I first saw my son's little body, I felt so many things. I felt anger, because God could have stopped it. I say this as kindly as I can, but you have to be delusional to think he can't stop your tragedy. Because he can. Obviously, I felt sadness, because no matter what anyone says, what anyone does, where I go, how many more kids I have, Henry is gone. My little boy who kicked and played in my womb is gone. Just like that. And for a while, a long while, I walked around feeling all these things. Mad. Sad. Picked on. Bitter. Singled out for a price I didn't deserve to pay.

I've mentioned before that I'm a social worker. In my work I've seen sexually abused children returned to their abusers. I've seen kids malnourished because they were locked in the attic for weeks at a time. I really struggled to understand why these people got to keep babies they didn't even want when I had mine taken from me. People willingly harmed their children, but Jesus took my son? I followed all the health rules during my pregnancy, but I have friends who got drunk and chainsmoked while pregnant. And God took *my* child? For a long time, I would walk around and look at pregnant people, thinking, *Why not her?* That lady in front of me at Target. *Why not her?* That woman who once had an abortion. *Why not her?* I know I'm setting myself up for a lot of criticism as I admit this out loud, but I refuse to cover my pain, my anger, and my bitterness in fig leaves. I. Was. Raw.

I knew the "church answer" to all this. In fact, I'd given the church answer to many people. "What a ministry this will all be," an elderly lady told me at church. Truth is, I didn't give two cents about who my loss ministered to. If God had given me the choice of Henry surviving or one person coming to know Jesus because of his death, I'd choose Henry. I want you to understand the full weight of what I'm saying here. I wanted to wish this on someone besides me. I wanted to die. I didn't want God's story for me. I would go as far to say I didn't even want God's glory. I wanted my son. I wanted Benjamin to have his brother. I wanted to watch Henry go to kindergarten. I wanted to dance with him at his wedding. I wanted to do life with this boy who grew in my belly. And I felt robbed of all of that.

If you have experienced a loss like this, please hear nothing but deep, unwavering support as I continue. Because I don't want to sound like a cliché or like some optimistic twit who knows nothing of great pain. I'm saying these next words as someone who has experienced the pain of holding her dead child's body. We serve an amazingly awesome God. He is El Roi, "the God who sees." He is the God who sees *me*. He is the God who sees *you*. And that, my friends, is why he doesn't give us a choice when it comes to great suffering. He didn't give me the choice of Henry or no Henry. He doesn't give us the choice of cancer or no cancer. Of infertility or fertility. He doesn't let you decide if your husband leaves you or not. Do you know why? Because, like a typical child, we don't know what's best for us. We only see what we can see. We only decide on the facts in front of us. We don't see what he sees.

So, the other day, after baseball practice, my daughter saw a tiny little puddle and jumped and splashed to her heart's content. I looked over her shoulder and saw a massive puddle over the hill. This puddle was the big kahuna of all puddles. It had more mud and way more water. There were even a few other kids playing in it already. I grabbed her hand to lead her to the better puddle and she lost it. I mean, full-on psychotic breakdown. She couldn't see what I saw. She kicked and screamed and thrashed as I carried her to the mecca of all puddles. When I sat her down, she looked around and saw the better situation. The mud. The kids. The water. She took off running and played to her heart's content, never looking back.

This is exactly what God does for us. We may be splashing and having a ball in our tiny, little puddle, but God doesn't want that for us. He wants us in the mecca of all puddles. More mud. More water. Cool people to play with. He always has eternity in mind. He always sees beyond the horizon—over the hill, if you will. As humans, we know only of our momentary pain. Tiny puddles. Our heartaches. Our love as a parent. Our temporary circumstances. Our comfort. We don't see what he sees. And he loves us way too much to let us splash in tiny puddles. Why? Because that prayer you prayed when you were eight or twelve or even last year? He heard you. He actually took you seriously and he loves you too much to let you stay in mediocrity. Let him make you uncomfortable for your own good. Let him bless you. Let him take you to better places. To higher places.

We serve an amazingly awesome God. He is El Roi, "the God who sees." He is the God who sees me. He is the God who sees you. And that, my friends, is why he doesn't give us a choice when it comes to great suffering.

Frankly, I don't know how God did it. I don't know how God could send his son to die. To take on all our junk. To suffer so greatly. For us. For sinful people who love themselves more than him most days. I mean, that's huge! That's everything, and if God had changed his mind, like I so begged him to with my son, Henry wouldn't be singing glory with the angels right now. He'd be in hell, like the rest of us would be had God changed his mind. You see, God didn't yield, because he knew the cross had to happen, and no matter the pain, no matter how great the loss, he had one thing in mind: glory. And if he didn't change his mind watching Jesus cry out in agony, he isn't going to change his mind for you or me, either. And as much as it hurts, as much as it downright sucks, you don't want him to.

I believe worship is a choice. It's easy to jump up and down and lift your hands in praise when things are good, but how about when you're crushed? When God's perfect plan is offensive. When tears are all you have. When you lose all sense of reverence and scream at the Creator of the universe because he allowed something beyond comprehension to happen to you. Hear me when I say this. Hear me loud and clear. God is not bothered one iota by your screams. God is not shaken by the laments of your heart. In fact, he welcomes them. Like a mother welcomes a child into her lap after a holy fit, God welcomes you into his. Your gut-wrenching cries are actually a form of worship. You may feel stone cold. You may feel angry beyond words. But that doesn't change the character of God. Sister, your feelings don't change the steadfast love and character of God. I remember telling my mom that I felt like I was talking to a wall when I prayed. Her response: *Then lean on the wall, Baby.* You may feel angry. You may feel rage. You may feel like you have nothing to bring but anger and tears and unmet needs, but that's not true. You have authenticity. You have pain. You have surrender. Take that to him. He can handle it. He delights in your honesty.

People ask me all the time how I know God is real. Do you get that question? While part of me is tempted to open my Bible, I'm not sure how compelling that is to someone who doesn't yet believe it. But pain is compelling. People understand pain. They may not know Jesus, but my word, they also cannot argue with what he's done in you. Your story is powerful. It's moving. And it needs to be told. People will try to debate you over theology all day long, but the way Jesus has held you through your storms? That is a force to be reckoned with. No one can debate it. Tell your story. Your story is powerful.

I sometimes wonder why God allows so much suffering for one person and what seems like nothing for somebody else. In fact, I know quite a few people who appear to live as I once did, whose biggest struggle is having to work part time to pay for fun vacations. Or someone who can't decide if they should have four or five kids. The human in me wants to remind God that it's not fair. But deep down, deep, deep, deep down in my Jesus-loving soul, I feel sorry for them. They get the cheap end of the deal. Because if you really get the point of this life, if you really believe that this is but a moment—if you really understand the gospel and want to be like Christ, why would you balk at suffering? Why wouldn't you welcome it? Why wouldn't you be okay with being molded into Jesus?

Don't get me wrong, pain sucks. And in the midst of pain, I kick and scream and act like my daughter did when I yanked her from her tiny little puddle. But that's okay. We all grieve differently. There's no formula for how to suffer. Some of us stomp and lament. Others cry silently in their pillow. How you express your pain is irrelevant. Truth is, God doesn't care if you tear up gracefully like Jackie Kennedy or mourn like King David. He just wants your heart. And like any father, he is delighted when you crawl into his lap and cry. So, crawl into his lap. Crawl into his capable arms; let them envelop you with his perfect peace, and, sister, you just sit there as long as you need.

Weeping may last through the night, but joy comes with the morning.
Psalm 30:5b (NLT)

10

Sister, step aside.

*Leave it in the Hands that were
wounded for you.*
Elisabeth Elliot, Keep a Quiet Heart

I **HATE TO WATCH** people hurt. It literally makes my soul sick. Like
in the movie *Forrest Gump*. Do you remember that scene where Forrest gets on the school bus and no one will sit next to him? The words
"Seat's taken" haunt me. That has to be every mother's worst nightmare.
When your kid is left out. Pain. Loneliness. Bullying. It's not right, it's
just not. My kids are still pretty young, so I barely have skin in the game,
but I know their time is coming. Hardships, struggles, and life lessons
are all on the horizon. And as much as I'd like to fill my backpack with
their burdens, I can't. As much as I'd like to carry every single one of their
hardships throughout their precious lives, I can't. I can't and I shouldn't.
And you shouldn't either because it's not God's best for them.

Let me tell you about a woman in the Bible named Rebecca. She was
pretty cunning. Captivating. Strong, but beneath all that exterior, she had
a mother's heart. Rebecca was the mother of two twins named Jacob and
Esau. I mentioned them in chapter 5 when we talked about the things we
crave more than Jesus. Genesis 25:28 tells us that Esau was favored by his
father Isaac, but Rebecca favored Jacob. I'm not exactly sure what caused
each parent to have a favorite son, but here's my theory. Esau was the one

who loved the outdoors. He was a hunter. He and his father probably clicked on all things boy. Jacob, however, was more of an indoor guy. He was his mom's precious little boy that probably helped her around the house. At least that's what I imagine when I read Genesis 25:

> *When the boys grew up, Esau was a skillful hunter, a man of the field, while Jacob was a quiet man, dwelling in tents.*
>
> Genesis 25:27 (ESV)

My other guess is that Rebecca doted on Jacob so much because he was the underdog. Being your dad's number one and having his blessing was a huge deal in that era. The fact that Jacob didn't get the top spot is my guess as to why Rebecca favored him and, in my opinion, probably coddled him.

But what usually happens when we coddle our kids for too long? That's right. They become brats. They're usually difficult to be friends with and almost always have an air of entitlement. As parents, we don't set out to do that; we just hate to watch our kids hurt. We want to take away the pain so badly that sometimes we injure them in the process. And that's exactly what Rebecca did with Jacob. In her manipulative, cunning way, she tricked her blind husband into blessing Jacob instead of Esau. She had him put on Esau's clothes, make himself appear to be hairy (read all of Genesis 27 for the full story), and receive his father's blessing. When Esau learns of this switcheroo, he tries to kill Jacob, but guess what? His mommy helps him run away.

The story is very redemptive, and Jacob ends up being one heck of a dude, but I want to stop here to point out where I'm going with this story. Rebecca enabled her son Jacob. She didn't trust that God would bless him, so she took over and tried to bless him in her own way. Does this sound familiar to you at all? Trying to control outcomes? I'm just saying.

Now let's talk about Jacob for a minute. Let's talk about what a person becomes when they are raised without natural consequences. I bet Jacob was challenging to be around. I bet he was spoiled and pretty self-centered. Do you know people like that? Do you have a coworker who you avoid like the flu? Do you have a family member who you screen and only return their call with a text? I know I have some folks who probably screen my calls, and I have a couple of friends in mind right now who drive me bonkers. You know these people. They may be negative, or always have a problem. They might be needy, or just plain annoying. But here's the sobering part—the kick-in-the-pants part. Try being that person's mom. As manipulative and controlling as Rebecca was, I'm sure beneath it all, there was pain. Can you imagine how it must have felt to watch her son be second pick? It's the equivalent of watching your kid not get invited to a party. Or watching them sit at home on a Saturday night or skip prom because nobody asked them. I'm not there yet, but I know some of you are. I bet it's excruciating. And in that hurt, in that deep hurting for your child or friend, there's a good chance you have taken the word *grace* and run with it. Listen carefully. Grace is the most beautiful gift on the planet. Grace is undeserved mercy that cost God a hefty price and cost us nothing. Grace is truly amazing, but let me tell you what it is *not*. Grace is not trying to shoulder everyone else's burdens every day. Grace is not shielding our loved ones from pain. Grace is not fixing everything we can for our loved ones. In fact, grace does not require us to fix anything at all.

I know what you're probably thinking right now. *Isn't that the opposite of Scripture? Aren't there verses about carrying one another's burdens?* Actually, yes! Galatians 6:2 tells us to carry one another's burdens. So, yes, you are absolutely right. We are called, commanded even, to carry one another's burdens, but have you ever thought about what that really means? Carrying one another's burdens does not mean fixing everything. At a certain point, what we call grace isn't really grace anymore—it's enabling. Like Rebecca, I would do anything for my hurting child. Anything. But I'm pretty sure circumventing God's will or lying to my husband is not the best choice. Intervening to control outcomes is wrong, even if your motives are good. Think about it; how the heck do you think things will turn out if you have to sin to get there?

"But the Bible tells us to lift one another up," you say. Absolutely, it does. The Bible tells us to show up, to serve, to love. But what it does not say anywhere from Genesis to Revelation is to take away one another's pain. Not only is this impossible, but it circumvents the Lord's work in our lives. I have said on multiple occasions, I would inject pain from my loved ones directly into my own veins if it meant that suffering would bypass them. I bet you would, too. But that's not biblical. That's the antithesis of biblical. Carrying one another's burdens does not mean protecting one another from every hardship. In fact, if our support does anything but point someone to Jesus, we've crossed the line. If our support allows someone to escape natural consequences, to trust in someone other than Jesus, we are hurting them. Carrying one another's burdens must, at its core, point people to Jesus. I am going to say that again because I just want to. We must point each other to Jesus when we carry one another's burdens. Obviously, this looks different for each person. Only you and your spiritual counselors can process that, but I can assure you that Rebecca is not the only mom to have enabled her kid. We all do it. That's precisely why I'm writing this: for awareness, for accountability, and because *I* struggle with enabling.

As a mother, I see what enabling parents try to accomplish. We want to give our kids a good future. Sadly, sometimes we just want them to like us—to *need* us. We don't want one mistake to threaten that. Lying on a scholarship application, doing our kid's homework, covering up a drug addiction, supplying alcohol for a party—some of you are gasping right now, others may agree with some of these methods. But no matter where you camp on this issue, enabling sets your kids up for failure. Even done in love. Even done with the best of intentions, it produces the same result.

Rebecca set Jacob up for failure. What she did, what we do, debilitates our children. When we clean up our kids' messes, when we throw money and resources to make their life easy, when we use every bit of whatever power or influence we have to cushion our kids, this is detrimental to their growth. I know your intentions are good. I know you simply want your hurting child to see what you see: someone beautiful and capable of great things—but even with love at the root, you are making things worse. Why? Because you are sending them a message that they are incapable without your help. Rebecca did it. Celebrities do it. Politicians do it. Pastors do it. And we do it. Sadly, our attempts, no matter how well intended, send our kids running to us over and over again. To our calming words. To our money. To our support. To our validation. We become their safe place. We become their strong tower. When we carry our children's pain, when we fix their situation so that they don't have to suffer natural consequences, we point them to *us*, not to Jesus. I say this with a very heavy heart because I hope none of us mean to do this. I think most of us just want our kids to love God the way we do. As my kids age and I face the temptation to be their shield, may I always remember 1 Peter 4:11:

Do you have the gift of speaking? Then speak as though God himself were speaking through you. Do you have the gift of helping others? Do it with all the strength and energy that God supplies. Then every-thing you do will bring glory to God through Jesus Christ. All glory and power to him forever and ever! Amen.

1 Peter 4:11 (NLT)

We have to speak, serve, and love in his name and his name only—not in our own efforts and certainly not in our own strength—so that *God* gets the glory. Not us. Our kids are going to fall and that's okay. Every great person has the potential to fall—and to fall hard. But confidence in Jesus gives meaning to all of it. When we are weak, he is strong. His power is made perfect in weakness. Only Jesus can make suffering and weakness a good thing. Why? Because suffering and weakness points us to God—our creator. And with God, all things are possible. All things are bearable. Every bit of pain, struggle, weakness, and hardship has meaning. It is redemptive. We are better because of it. He is glorified because of it. This is a win-win situation. Don't be the reason your kids miss it. Don't be the reason your husband misses it. When we, as loving parents, friends, and sisters, attempt to alleviate suffering for our people, we circumvent Jesus.

One day God is going to ask something of them. One day, our kids are going to be stretched to the max and we need to know our place. We may have birthed these babies, we may be entrusted with them, to love and nurture them, but make no mistake: they belong to the Lord. It is our job to point them to a Savior who will redeem any situation life throws at them. That's love. That's grace. That trumps any effort to fix things.

Let's be honest. This helping-versus-enabling thing is a very fluid line, it's also very tricky because enabling looks like love. It acts like love. It is very closely related to love, only it's *not* love. So what exactly is enabling? Enabling is doing something *for* someone that they can do themselves, for example, our kids' homework. I know this is a very simple example, but enabling usually starts off in small ways. Your kid may need some guidance on their English essay or math homework. I get that some kids may need more direction than others, but the bottom line is that it's *their* work. We can help them by encouraging them, giving them the tools, supplies, and space they need or maybe get them outside help so that they can do it themselves, but that's it. Because one day, y'all, one day our kiddos will have a college essay or a project at work. One day our kids will mess up or someone might betray them. And guess what? Mommy won't be there to bail them out. As much as I'd like to, I can't. We can't.

Allow me to be frank with you. Enabling creates a dependency on us that is not only arrogant but also creates idolatry. You may think you're helping. You may love the mess out of someone. You may think you're being selfless, but really, if you're enabling them, you are causing them to bow down and worship you. Yeah, I know. Pretty blunt but we have to sober up on this issue, so I said it. I said it so I don't make the mistake of teaching my kids to bow down to me. I said it so I don't ask the poor to bow down to me. I said it so I don't ask a friend to bow down to me. I said it so I can be held accountable. Because my purpose, my sole purpose on this earth is to point people to Jesus. That's it. There's nothing else more important. Nothing. When you carry burdens not meant for you, you are not pointing people to Jesus. You're pointing them to yourself. You're actually circumventing their need for a real Savior. I know it's probably unintentional, but whether intentional or not, you're hurting them. You're patronizing them. You're being condescending. You're one-upping. And in that process, you're shaming the one in need. Why? Because you're not allowing someone the chance to rise up in the strength of their Lord. You aren't helping them create tools and coping mechanisms. You're actually creating a false dependency on you. You're crippling the very people you love.

Listen, I'm not saying that you ditch someone in a dark time, that you throw a "there, there" at them and go on with your business. Hardly! In fact, I've walked through some dark places with people glued to my hip. I've been held together in some dark places by family and godly counsel who pointed me to Jesus. I may have held their hand for a long time, but I was being walked toward a Savior. My Savior. And if you ask me, walking hand in hand toward the cross with hurting people is real biblical love.

**When you carry burdens not meant for you, you
are not pointing people to Jesus. You're actually
circumventing their need for a real Savior.**

———————

This enabling thing is a slippery slope. It starts with rescuing your kids when they forget their homework at school for the third time. Then it becomes calling a judge who can make a violation go away. Then it becomes giving an adult child so much money that they turn to you to provide instead of working hard themselves or leaning on their spouse. I love what Dr. Henry Cloud and Dr. John Thompson say in their book *Boundaries* (Zondervan, 2017): *"To rescue people from the natural consequences of their behavior is to render them powerless."* In your current situation, are you helping someone avoid the natural consequences of their mistakes? Are you cushioning their fall? Are you the barrier to the rug being pulled out from under them? Because if you are, if this is you, you are handicapping them. I urge you to let God pull the rug out from under the person you love most. I know it's hard. I know it's scary, but I promise you that he loves them more than you do. After all, he died for them.

I feel like we know in our heads that enabling is bad, but our hearts still struggle with the concept. I mean, why on earth do we do this? Why do we swoop in and attempt to take over? Why do we shield our loved ones from natural consequences? I'm pretty sure the answer is rooted in unbelief. The bottom line is that we don't trust God to move in the lives of those we love the most. At least I don't. Before I continue, let me remind you that I am aware that people are dealing with some really hard stuff. We love our people so much. We want all the good things this life has to offer them. When they hurt, we hurt. When it comes to my kids, I feel this so deeply. Even in their big, adult mistakes, I will probably still see the young girl who wasn't asked to the party or the young boy who didn't make the baseball team. I can tell you this much. If I'm not pointing my children to Jesus, the one who died for them, then I'm wrong. I'm wrong when they are five. I'm wrong when they're fifty. Leading them to the one who died for them should never be option B. I know you love them, but your love pales in comparison to the love of God.

Sisters, not everything that weighs us down is ours to carry. On the contrary. It's ours to pray about. It's ours to process with a therapist or with a church leader who can come alongside and offer godly support. But it's not ours to carry. Hebrews 12:10 says that God disciplines us for our good. Why? Because he wants us to be holy. He wants our children to be holy. And in that process, he allows people to experience hardship and consequences for mistakes. He can't do that if we're in the way. So, get out of the way. I know you mean well, but my stars, you are paralyzing your loved ones. Truth is, they may get to the end of this life and not know Jesus because *you* replaced their Savior. This makes me shudder. I mean absolutely shudder. Do you hear what I'm saying? The people you love the most may want to know Jesus, but if you're always saving them time and time again, then guess what? They only know you. They are bowing down to you. You, my friend, may be standing in the way of knowing the Savior of the world. Of their walking with him. Of their abiding in him. And here is the awful reality. You may offer some protection in this difficult world. You may offer love, friendship, and security, but in reality, you may be just hastening their plummet to hell. Step aside, my friend. Step aside, scared mama. You and I just don't know more than God about what's best for his children.

The salvation of the righteous is from the Lord; *he is their stronghold in the time of trouble.*

                                                            Psalm 37:39 (ESV)

11

Sister, teach them.

My mom loves Jesus.
My son Benjamin

I **ONCE REFERRED TO** my boys as Beavis and Butt-Head in the
Target parking lot. The sweet mom next to me might have had a car-
diac event. Then there was the time I threw a juice cup to Samuel
while he was at the top of the stairs because I was too lazy to walk it up
to him. Naturally, it hit him square in the mouth and busted his lip open.
The countless times my sons have peed in cups in the car should be a
crime. And the time my son said "gross" when he saw my lady parts?
After telling him it was his choice to walk into my room, I reminded
him that it was these lady parts that pushed him into existence. I've been
doing this mom thing long enough to realize there are two types of families. Occasionally, there's crossover, but for the most part you fall into
one or the other: sweet or salty.

Sweet families. The world needs more sweet families. These are the
kinds of families that attend story time at the library because they actually speak with inside voices. And like books for that matter. Their homes
have lamps and china cabinets and all things white. Why? Because
they're calm when it's appropriate. They're not sissies per se. They just
understand indoor etiquette. And the matriarch of a sweet family? Wow.
Just wow. She's usually well put together in an Audrey Hepburn kind

of way. A dear friend of mine is one of these mothers, and I couldn't think more highly of her. I don't think she's ever raised her voice, and I know for a fact she's never farted. I know this to be true because her son confirmed this for me. And before you accuse her of being heavily medicated or some sort of a Stepford wife, I assure you she's not. She's genuine and sweet. Like Godiva chocolate. The real deal. Her kids wear Polo and Lilly Pulitzer and take family pictures on their porch. She even refers to bathroom breaks as "going to the restroom," and I'm pretty sure none of her kids pick their nose. She's not perfect, but she definitely appears that way. I imagine her asking her husband to take the trash out with the words "please" and "sweetheart" in front of her simple request. I have learned so much from this friend. I love being around her. The world needs women and families like hers.

Then there's the salty type. I could write a novel on these types of families. Salty folks, y'all. They aren't for the faint of heart. These are the kinds of people who have two volumes: loud and louder. There's usually a lot of sarcasm and bathroom humor mixed with some very heated fellowship. We're not sinful in our salty ways, necessarily. I mean, last I checked it wasn't a sin to feed boogers to your dog. And the parents of these families? Definitely interesting folks. There's usually a "pull my finger" father and a mother who screams things like, "What the b-hole" in the car line. (I'm just assuming.) Not that all salty folks have potty mouths. They're just open. I imagine most salty folks pee with the door wide open. Salty kids are no different either. They write things like "poop" and "butt" on the back of their grandmother's dirty windshield without her noticing and laugh as she drives off to Bible study. (So I've heard.) These kids give each other wedgies and knock over lamps. After all, they have no awareness of indoor etiquette. And while they are intense and a tad "spirited," these families are fun. The world needs more salty people too. My sweet friends love being around my salty family.

Truth is, neither is right nor wrong. Both have a place in this world. Can you imagine a bunch of sweet people living together with no salt? It's like chips without dip. Or pie with no ice cream. Or what about a bunch of salty folks? Can you imagine the chaos? Both are needed in this thing called life. Both are welcome. Both have a seat at the table. And guess what? God delights in both kinds of people.

Think about your own personality or family dynamic. Are you reserved or demonstrative? Do you prefer Superman or "Ring Around the Rosie"? Do you make your kids wear collared shirts to school or are you a "whatever is clean" kind of girl? Do you refer to your backside as a "bottom" or "booty" or do you just call it an old-fashioned "butt"? What's your tone at the dinner table? Wherever you land on the spectrum, it doesn't matter. I mean it does a little, but in the grand scheme of things, being sweet or salty makes no difference. The only thing that matters in this whole parenting game is that you teach your tiny humans the radical love of Jesus. Period. And if anyone tells you otherwise, if anyone tries to box your style or criticizes your methods of teaching your kids the gospel, they can kiss your butt. Or booty. Hear me loud and clear when I say this. If you ever feel like you should be a little more this or a little less that in your attempts to teach your kids about Jesus, turn that noise off. I don't care if it's the voice of your precious mother or some jerk at Target, they don't get a vote. Jesus entrusted those babies to you. He trusts you.

My husband and I had dinner with some friends a few months ago, and of course we talked about our children. What else do people with kids in their thirties talk about when their kids aren't around? This couple is pretty hardcore in the best of ways. No sugar. No soda. No food after 8:00 p.m. Their kids read every day and are allowed one hour of screen time a day, even in the summer. No YouTube. No sleeping in each other's beds. Private school. Honor Society. Piano lessons. They are every bit of parenting I'm not. My husband and I listened intently but dared not speak for fear they would call Child Protective Services on the spot. Bed stealers. Bed wetters. Sugar. YouTube. Bus riders. It's how we roll.

On the way home from dinner I started reflecting on the conversation. Am I a good mom? My kids drink soda. They love to play on my phone too. And sugar? I gave them Lucky Charms in bed last night. Was I wrong to let Samuel ride the school bus at five years old? Maybe we should do private school. Am I a naive Christian because they go to public school? Maybe we should take the TV out of their room. Do they read enough? Do they read ever? Crap. Do they know how to read? That's when the Holy Spirit piped up. Not audibly. I'm not Moses. God has yet to talk to me through a burning bush, but his still small voice was loud enough to redirect my downward spiral. While God and I didn't really have a direct exchange, it went something like this:

"Daughter, do you teach your kids about me?"

"Yes."

"Do they see you read your Bible? Do you pray with them?"

"Yes and yes."

"Do you take them to church?"

"Yes."

"Do they see Jesus in you?"

"Yes."

"Is there anything more important in your home than their loving me and my people?"

"No."

"Then why do you compare your parenting to others?"

I came home and read Deuteronomy to ease my humanity:

So commit yourselves wholeheartedly to these words of mine. Tie them to your hands and wear them on your forehead as reminders. Teach them to your children. Talk about them when you are at home and when you are on the road, when you are going to bed and when you are getting up. Write them on the doorposts of your house and on your gates, so that as long as the sky remains above the earth, you and your children may flourish in the land the Lord swore to give your ancestors.

Deuteronomy 11:18–21 (NLT)

While I've come to terms with the fact that I am a little unconventional in my parenting style, I still have my bouts with insecurity in all of it. Is that a salty thing or do sweet moms deal with this as well? Send me to a mom's group, and I'm as scared as a toddler about to get shots. It is like "Facing Goliath" intimidating. And don't even get me started on class parties. I get out-Pinterested every time. Then there's the fact that I work part time, so I don't feel like I quite fit in with the stay-at-home moms. When I had my first child, I wasn't sure what was wrong with me. For example, I hated play dates. In fact, I still do. I'd rather go to Target or play in a pile of dirt and just do life with my kids. Scheduled fun is not for me. Going to Chick-fil-A and watching the kiddos play while I chatted with their friends' moms left me tired. I assumed I was just being selfish, so I kept trying. The children's museum. MOPS. Story time. I amped it up, but nothing changed. I would see all these smiling, refreshed moms coming out of these places, and I was exhausted—and disappointed in myself. I couldn't understand why we had to go to the zoo in a massive group. And what was the all the rage about Kinder Music? Truth is, I was lonely in this role. Even when I was with my friends on these play dates, I was so distracted with my kid that I could barely be present. How is this hanging out? Shouldn't we just go to dinner without kids? But I didn't tell anybody. For a while. Probably too long. My attitude felt wrong and bratty. And mostly I was ashamed. I had this incredible opportunity to stay home with my baby, and I didn't even want it. I wanted to be back at work. After leaving the park one day, I called my sister in tears. I felt like the most selfish human on the planet and it was time to confess. I braced myself for impact because I was about to be put in my place. Only she didn't do that. In fact, her words remain etched on my heart to this day.

"Why are you trying to deny your wiring?" she said. I was silent because, at first, I thought it was a trap.

"Kim, why are you suppressing God's calling for you to use your gifts?" Okay. I didn't see that one coming. She went on to remind me of something that I'd forgotten. Something so simple that I threw it aside under the pressure of what I thought was expected of me. She reminded me that God created me specifically and uniquely. His design is not flawed. And in that design, he created me to want to work. He gave me the particular gifts and tools I needed for my calling, which was in my work. To deny that yearning would be to deny my gifts. Now let me say it back to you.

Stay-at-home moms, God created you with unique gifts. Whether you stay home and care for your kids by choice or out of necessity, you are amazing and there is worth in what you are doing. You are using your particular gifts exactly where the creator of the universe wants you. God ordained this for you today, in this season. Bask in it.

Working moms, God created you with unique gifts. Whether you work outside the home by choice or out of necessity, you are amazing and there is worth in what you're doing. You are using your particular gifts exactly where the creator of the universe wants you. God ordained this for you today, in this season. Bask in it.

Truth be told, I would be denying who I am had I not returned to work part time. I wouldn't be happy, and I certainly wouldn't be writing this to you. I have found my balance and my groove in this parenting thing. I'm a better mom for it. I love my kids better for it. I serve Jesus better for it. But that's just me.

What about you? In the midst of work and play dates and raising kids, are you using your gifts? At home? At work? How are you bringing glory to Jesus where he has you? Are you working because you want more stuff? Are you working to provide for your family? Do you feel the call to quit? Do you want to work but fear mom shame? Do you need a better work situation? I don't know your story. I wish I did, but since I don't, I'm going to need you to do something for me. I need you to self-reflect as I ask you a series of questions:

Does your life reek of Jesus everywhere you go?

Does Jesus radiate from you as you go to work or on play dates?

Do your kids notice your love for Jesus?

Does your work glorify God?

If not, what needs to change?

Is God calling you to work?

Is God calling you to stay home?

Does something need to change?

I don't care if you're a heart surgeon or a stay-at-home mom, God gave you those babies to teach, to raise as disciples, and to love the mess out of *your* way. He entrusted *you* with their sweet souls for a reason. Don't look right or left and compare yourself to someone else. Salty people don't need to try and be sweet. Sweet people don't need to try and be salty.

When I became a mom, I looked to my sister-in-law for everything. I fed my kids solids when she told me to. I introduced milk when she did. I changed my kids' nap schedules when she said it was age appropriate. Literally, she could have told me to do ten jumping jacks, spin around five times, and stand on my head before putting my kids to bed and I would have done it. She was my Yoda. For the first few years of parenting I truly believed that my kids would've been better off with her. After all, her daughter was singing "Trust and Obey" at, like, three. At that time, my kid could barely talk. But then something happened. My five-year-old son wrote the words "My mom loves Jesus" in my journal. He didn't tell me. In fact, I'm not sure when he did this. But the day I opened the page I cried. I cried because that insecurity, the questioning of my methods, the obsessing over if we prayed that night or memorized a Bible verse that day—y'all, *it all went away.* That day I realized that my methods work too.

My sister-in-law is amazing and her kids are awesome, but my kids aren't better off with her. In fact, she told me that she had the same insecurities as I did. They just looked different. Whereas I cried and ran around like a chicken with my head cut off, she clung to order and structure. She told me that she craved affirmation that she was doing something right. And guess what? She was. She is.

I'm the mom Jesus picked for Benjamin, Samuel, and Sydney. She's the mom God picked for her kids. And you are the mom God picked for your kids. There is no right or wrong way to teach them to love Jesus. There's just personality difference. It doesn't matter if you say prayers at night or on the fly, just pray with your children. Teach them to talk to their Father. It doesn't matter if you take your kids to Saturday night church or Sunday morning services. Teach them to worship. Show them that you love to worship too. It doesn't matter if you read your Bible or listen to it on audio, teach them the gospel. Let them see you loving God's Word. Your method doesn't matter. It's your consistency. It's your devotion. It's the heart of your actions. That's how you infuse the gospel in your children. You don't need to try to make it cool or legalistic—or someone else's responsibility. You just practice what you preach.

Maybe I talk louder than most. Maybe I allow my kids to say "butt." Maybe we burp and pee with the door open. Maybe I put them in public school. But when they are standing face to face with Jesus, do you think it will matter? Do you think Jesus will ask them for their résumé? Sweet families like my friend love Jesus. But guess what? Salty families like mine love Jesus too. And both sweet and salty folks have the capacity to love Jesus and make him known to their children.

The friend I told you about who I had dinner with a few months ago? The one who doesn't allow soda or screen time? Her kids may run this country one day, but guess what? She doesn't take them to church. Or teach them about Jesus. So, while there's a good chance they will go to an Ivy League school and have great wealth, here's a 100 percent chance that they will stand before Jesus. I don't know about you, but I'd rather my kids work at McDonald's or go to technical college than to not know Jesus. Our goal as parents is not to teach our kids to be successful. I mean, you can, you should, but that should pale in comparison to the ultimate goal of teaching them to love and serve a great God.

> *Train up a child in the way he should go; even when he is old he will not depart from it.*
>
> Proverbs 22:6 (ESV)

12

Sister, choose holiness.

*The destined end of man is not happiness,
nor health, but holiness.*

Oswald Chambers,
My Utmost for His Highest

WE LIVE IN a culture that joneses on happiness, always pursues more. Happiness has become the idol of our generation. Privilege has become entitlement. Everything is up for grabs no matter the cost. And nothing, I mean, nothing should get in our way. After all, it's our right to be happy? YOLO (you only live once) and self-love, right? Your marriage is tough? YOLO, peace out, or just have an affair? I mean, that or be miserable. And if you're miserable why wouldn't you just leave? You could travel the world and go find yourself, that is, apart from the person you made a vow to love until the day you die. Work hard. I mean, kill it at the office so you can get that Louis bag you deserve. And a pedicure every two weeks. That's self-care, right? And that million-dollar home you can barely afford. Absolutely, you need it. Who cares if it means you and your spouse work long hours and send your kids home on the daycare bus. After all, you're doing it for their future so that they, too, can have all the things life has to offer. Oh, and don't forget to take vacations to places like Fiji and Disney World every year. It's for the kids, right? But you aren't without a soul. You're obviously going to take 10 percent off your paycheck (after taxes of course) and throw it in the offering plate. Or give it to charity.

This pursuing happiness stuff sounds great coming out of the mouth of an influencer or celebrity Christian who throws in a Jeremiah 29:11 here and there. It almost sounds believable to those claiming belief in a higher power, but it's problematic to the Christian faith. Before I go on, please note that I'm not knocking big houses or Louis bags. In fact, I have a few bucket list items of my own. I have this dream of my three kids in the back seat of our Jeep Rubicon. We cruise around town listening to '90s pop music (if I have my way). After getting snow cones or lattes or whatever we're in to, we'll drive up to our house. Nothing fancy. Just enough space to spread our stuff out comfortably. I'll have twinkle lights in the backyard and grass. Lots of thick Bermuda grass. My husband and I will sit on the patio and watch our kids play for hours. We'll talk. We'll laugh. We'll drink coffee or wine. Just writing it has my heart going pitter-patter.

Maybe my dream seems shallow to you. Maybe it seems noble compared to yours, I don't know. But I do know that my dream is not a biblical promise. Don't get me wrong. It's not wrong to have this dream. It's not immoral either, but I'm not entitled to it. Like I won't find a verse I can claim as I pray for it. I just want it. Will it make me happy? Sure, for a while. But my Jeep, my home with twinkle lights, my Bermuda grass, none of it touches the way of Jesus. Before you write me off, let me explain. Wanting more for your kids is a good thing. Having a nice setup to host your friends and neighbors is a good thing. Giving your children opportunities is an incredible gift, and, yes, it takes hard work to get there. But it's all fleeting. Much like a sugar high, none of these things will sustain you. Everything stales eventually. Every single dream you and I have, every single thing we want has a shelf life. Everything, that is, except the gospel. And if you drink the happiness Kool-Aid—the yummy, sugary, YOLO, self-love garbage—it will have you crashing in no time. What is it they say about champagne? Perfume going in, trash coming out. That's happiness. And if you're not careful, you will get so caught up in the American dream that you will live a life pursuing heaven on earth. Y'all, if you're pursuing earthly things, you're missing the things of heaven. Eternal things. Heavenly minded things. You may even stop pursuing Jesus altogether.

A friend of mine texted me the other day about how lukewarm Christianity is so prevalent that it's scary. For those of you who aren't familiar with this term, it basically means you don't burn for Jesus yet you claim to be a Christian. You may go to church. You may even be in a Bible study, but you haven't really been transformed by the gospel. I wanted to agree with my friend except I don't think I believe in the term. I knew the point she was trying to make, but it's an oxymoron in my opinion. To me, you're either saved or you aren't. You either follow Christ or you don't. You either hate your sin or you don't. I have this new sense of urgency to wake up proclaiming believers because I'm starting to think some of the people who claim Jesus may not really know him. Please do not miss this next part.

I am in no way condemning anyone here. I would never presume to tell you who knows the Lord and who doesn't. But I will say this with a heavy, serious, grace-filled heart. If you identify as a Christian only by going to church or by your actions, then I want you to really self-reflect here. If you identify as a Christian by your upbringing, morality, or the fact that you were baptized as a kid, I'm begging you to dig deeper here. Because here's the deal. The mark of a Christian is a personal relationship with Jesus Christ. And in that relationship, there's a conviction of sin. There's a transformation from the inside out. Not the other way around. I'm not saying that we always confess and repent. Heck, sometimes we live in sinful patterns for years, so don't hear what I'm not saying. In fact, I'm actually done saying and want to ask you the most important question of your life. Do you know Jesus? Apart from who your parents are. Apart from your behavior. Apart from how much knowledge you have or don't have. Do you have a personal relationship with Jesus Christ?

Even as a Christian, I think so many of us worship other gods more than we realize. I especially think we worship the pursuit of happiness. It's become the god of this culture while suffering seems to be a thing of the past. In fact, suffering is seen as a reason to reject God. Sadly, the phrase "holiness over happiness" has become archaic even to Christians. Think about it. When something goes south in our lives, we immediately get defensive. We question God's goodness and perhaps his existence because deep down we feel entitled to happiness. "I deserve it," we tell ourselves. After all, we follow Jesus. We should be comfortable. We deserve to be happy. We deserve to have nice things. But nowhere, I mean nowhere, is this in the Bible. Where in the Bible does it say that Jesus lived a comfortable life? Y'all, he was born in a stable. He was a carpenter. He didn't have money. He didn't have a palace like most kings. He certainly didn't have the applause of the crowd. Where does it say that God just wanted him to be happy? Nowhere. He was born for a purpose. And that purpose included being crucified. Nails in the wrists and feet while he slowly suffocated. While he took on our sin, alone, after asking God to find another way. Sisters, nowhere, I mean *nowhere* in the passion story does God have YOLO in mind. Nowhere in the Bible does it say anything about happiness. In fact, happiness isn't even on God's radar, because he doesn't want us just to be happy. I mean, it can be a by-product of certain circumstances, but the God of the Bible, that God, does not want you happy. No, girl. The God of the Bible wants us to be holy.

While I'd like to say that this doesn't apply to me, I can't. Especially when it comes to my children. The other day my son was telling me about some punk on the bus that said something hurtful. Before he could finish his story, I blasted the kid, his mother, and basically everything connected to this little jerk. It's as if someone took over my body. Y'all, I was ready to crush this poor kid and his dog because he said my kid's Pokémon card was stupid and stole his fidget spinner. That's how quickly my values went out the window when it came to protecting my child's happiness. Most of you get the mama bear thing, and while it appears noble, it can actually come back to bite you in the rear. What if your son comes to you one day, miserable in his marriage to some chick you never liked to begin with and says, "Mom, I'm not happy"? What if he tells you through teary eyes that he can't make it for fifty years and that he made a mistake? Or what if your daughter chooses friends or a lifestyle contrary to the gospel? What if she brings home an atheist who loves the mess out of her but not Jesus? I can endure hardships. I can understand God's grace in *my* suffering. But my children? They are off-limits, right? Mama, I know you would give your children both your kidneys. Run into a burning building. Swim into a dang shark's mouth! I know you would take all their hits, absorb all their pain, but, is this really love? Is allowing our kids to walk a path where we shield them from suffering really love?

The answer is a big fat no. Telling God that our children are off-limits, that their happiness trumps holiness, does them such a great disservice.

It basically hijacks the Lord's perfect plan and puts matters into our own hands. It circumvents God's sovereignty over their lives, because we act as if we know what's best for them. In fact, happiness can change like the flip of a light switch. Think about it. You can have the greatest day, come home, fight with your spouse, and suddenly your day sucks. I know this is a simple example, but think about it. Think about the things you wanted five years ago. Do those things still make you happy? For me the answer is no. My Joanna Gaines kitchen is the perfect example of fleeting happiness. Five years ago we moved into a fixer-upper and I went for it in the kitchen. I had just left Texas where Chip and JoJo were all the rage. White everything. Yes please!

Only I hate everything about it now. Especially the white cabinets. I see dirt. I see dust. They're also chipped from the many baths I gave my kiddos in the farmhouse sink. The *white* farmhouse sink that's kind of cream colored now. And the pale grey walls. I literally find a booger or mud on the walls daily. All I want is to paint my kitchen a darker color, or redo my cabinets with a stained wood. That white kitchen that once made me so happy now makes me cringe. Listen to me. Happiness changes day to day, usually based on our feelings. Our souls weren't created to live off happiness. It's just not sustainable. If you don't believe me, let me point you to Gethsemane. Jesus prayed to his Father. No, he pleaded to his daddy to take his cup of suffering. "*Father, if you are willing, please take this cup of suffering away from me. Yet I want your will to be done, not mine.*" (Luke 22:42 NLT). How do you think God felt as he heard the anguished cries of his one and only son?

Yet in his prayers, in his gut-wrenching, honest prayers, Jesus said, "*Yet I want your will to be done, not mine.*" That we could be so bold, so eternally minded, for our children and our friends. You see, God knew the weight of what Christ was asking, just like he knows the weight of what we are asking. For ourselves, for our spouses, and for our children. We do ourselves and our children unspeakable harm when we try to short-circuit what God intends for glory. I know we mean well. I know we are trying to love them well. But, y'all, the God who created the universe knows best. He is all knowing. You and I just can't compete with that.

I don't say any of these things lightly. I am speaking as someone who has suffered. As a mother who held her dead son after a stillbirth. As someone who wanted happiness more than anything. As a daughter who once saw suffering as something cruel from a God she so loved. I can't imagine what my parents were thinking as they watched me lament. As my husband heard my screams instead of Henry's cries when he was delivered. When my mom watched me curl into a ball in his nursery and pray to go home too. Don't think for one second she wouldn't have taken my pain into her own soul if she could? But she knew better. And you know what? I want to know better for my kids too. I want to know that the safest, most joyful place they can be is in God's will, even if it means they are suffering for a moment—or a season. I want to remember that God loves them more than I do and that their joy comes from him—not from anything I can give them in this world. I'm tired of watching Christian parents be okay with sin in order to make their kids happy. The pursuit of happiness will not heal us or our kids. Only the pursuit of Jesus Christ can do that.

We do ourselves and our children unspeakable harm when we try to short-circuit what God intends for glory.

I'd like to say I've grasped this lesson because I'm so godly, but may I remind you that I once prayed that my husband would die. I've already admitted this to you once, but I'm telling you again because it was my honest prayer in a very unhappy season, a season where I wanted my needs met by my husband and they weren't, a season where I wasn't sure if my marriage would get better. In a season where my husband was selfish, yes, but where I made him solely responsible for my self-declared entitlement to happiness. I'm not sure if God laughed at my bold honesty or wept over my sinful heart, but amen that he is not consumed with making his children happy. Hallelujah that he let me stay in a seemingly hopeless situation, only to redeem it and make it beautiful. And the whole time that I was miserable in my marriage, my mother did not once tell me to chase happiness. She did not once tell me to leave because I had my whole life ahead of me. She never uttered the words "I just want you to be happy." Nope. She was on her knees praying for my holiness and pointing me back to Christ, just as her mother taught her and just as

I want to teach my children. Sisters, we have to pray this for our babies. We have to bless the next generation and point them to Jesus because the world is feeding us sugar.

As my kids get closer to adolescence, I feel an urgency more than ever to lead them toward holiness. It's too important. And if God pointed his own son to glory, why wouldn't I do the same? Why wouldn't I want the same? This life is fleeting. Seriously, just yesterday I was cruising to cheer practice in my old Ford Explorer listening to Britney Spears. Now I'm forty and driving my daughter to gymnastics while listening to Kidz Bop. And before I know it, I'll be standing face to face with the King. Life goes that fast. And at the finish line, whenever that may be, I know that I know that I know that I will not regret choosing holiness in my parenting, in my friendships, in my marriage, and for myself. Even if it means I don't get my Jeep. Or twinkle lights. Even if it means I watch my children struggle. Or that I stay in my marriage when it gets rough. Because one day this precious life will be a thing of the past. You and I will be in the ground. And guess what? Twinkle lights and fancy vacations won't matter one bit. The only thing, and I mean *the only thing* that will have mattered is that we chose holiness.

Praise the Lord!
Blessed is the man who fears the Lord, who greatly delights in his commandments!

Psalm 112:1 (ESV)

13

Sister, burn!

*Darling, you can either burn for
the world or for Christ.*
Robyn Sarah-Lee Adams

I **RECENTLY READ THE** quote "I love Jesus but I cuss a little." I'll be
honest. This doesn't sit well with me. Not because I think cussing is a
sign of damnation. I said a cuss word just the other day. I bumped my
head on a cabinet, and my first reaction was to utter a four-letter word
under my breath. It happens, so please don't stop reading and label me
as a stuck-up Pharisee who judges cursers. I just find it irreverent to act
like it's no big deal when one flies out of your mouth. Because it is a big
deal. It's a sin, and sin is a big deal. I have read multiple Christian authors
who cuss in their books and on social media. Not when they tripped or
hit a curb with their car. Nope. They thought about it. They typed it out.
They sent it to print. It's like they are blatantly trying to make a point that
cussing is culturally accepted.

We all do this to some extent. Drinking. Eating. Spending. We have
all accepted cultural norms in some capacity and failed to hold them
next to truth. I'll even admit that I see the message trying to be conveyed
when people say, "I love Jesus but I cuss a little." I really do. It's a come-
as-you-are statement. And I love come-as-you-are statements. "Come as
you are" is the essence of Jesus. It's just like him to say it doesn't matter

if you're gay, straight, Black, White, fat, skinny, rich, or poor. Come eat with me. Come do life with me. Come with your sin. Come with your brokenness. This gives me chills just to write. Jesus is the epitome of love in spite of our imperfections. But that's not the message being conveyed here. This mentality, this "I love Jesus but cuss a little" motto comes across as complacent to me. It lacks conviction. And here's the deal. You either feel a conviction for your sin or you don't. And, sister, if you don't burn for Jesus, if you have become numb to the conviction of the Holy Spirit, then you have become complacent. And remember what I said at the very beginning of this book: complacency and Christianity don't make sense when used together. Revelation 3:15–16 says: *"I know your deeds, that you are neither cold nor hot. I wish you were either one or the other! So, because you are lukewarm—neither hot nor cold—I am about to spit you out of my mouth."* Are you hot or are you cold? Are you all in or all out? Because here's the deal. Lukewarm doesn't work for Jesus. That's not a thing.

My mom once told me a metaphor of a frog in a pot when I was in high school. I'm sure you've all heard it, but if you haven't, humor me. If you throw a frog in a pot of boiling water, what's it going to do? Jump out. Duh. Who wouldn't? But if you place a frog in a pot of warm water and slowly, strategically, crank up the heat, what will happen? You guessed it. Frog legs for dinner. That's exactly what complacency is to the Christian life. Sneaky. A back door to deception. It's a slippery slope. It's comfortable and sounds good, but don't be fooled. It's wicked. So wicked, in fact, that it misleads people into thinking they know a Savior who does not claim them. This gives me nightmares. So much so that I'm willing to say all the hard things and put myself out there for criticism if it means you will really hear me when I say this again. Sister, you either burn for Jesus or you don't. There is no in-between.

While "I love Jesus but I cuss a little" may be an innocent quote for a coffee cup, it lacks struggle. How about "I love Jesus but I struggle with cussing," or "I love Jesus but I struggle with drinking too much"? Or "I love Jesus but I struggle with being a good wife"? In all honesty, whatever your struggle, it should be just that: a struggle. And, if you identify yourself as a Christian you should be struggling with sin. With your flesh. With your natural leanings. Every single day. That's the work of the Holy Spirit inside you. He convicts you of your sin. And while there's no condemnation for those who know him, the Spirit in your soul should cause an unsettling in your soul when things aren't right. A frustration. Paul describes the struggle so accurately in Romans 7:15:

> *For I do not understand my own actions. For I do not do what I want, but I do the very thing I hate.*
>
> Romans 7:15 (ESV)

See the tension here? The struggle to want to stop sinning. And I'm sorry/not sorry, but "I love Jesus but I cuss a little" cheapens the struggle. It redefines the call to holy living. Christian, don't compromise here. I don't care if you think saying a few bad words is not as serious as cheating on your spouse or if drinking a bottle of wine every night is better than cheating on your taxes. It doesn't matter if you think watching trash on Netflix is better than hard-core porn. The world is not our litmus test for right and wrong—the Bible is. The way Jesus walked this earth is. And if you aren't struggling with sin, if there's no wrestling in your heart with it, I say this in complete love and longing for your soul: You might not have the Holy Spirit living in you. And if you don't, you might not know Jesus. I'm not saying this to condemn you. I'm saying this because Christ came to save you. In fact, nothing matters to me more than you knowing and accepting what Jesus did for you, than your understanding that you can struggle daily with sin and still be his! But—as someone who has an overwhelming passion to share the gospel—I have to say this again: if you don't wrestle with sin, you may not be a Christian. And I want you to know Jesus. I want you to know him so badly that I could come out of this page. This is why I am asking you these hard things. Sister, I will put my heart out there if it helps you want to know him. I will take the criticism. I will take the push back, anything, but ultimately, it's not up to me.

Are you hot or are you cold? Are you all in or all out? Because here's the deal. Lukewarm doesn't work for Jesus. That's not a thing.

Truth is, it's up to you. If you feel a wrestling, I want you to know that the tension has a name. It's the Holy Spirit—and he is wooing you. Don't fight him. He is calling you toward something more. And before you tell me why you can't take that step, let me stop you. No one is good enough. No one will ever be good enough. Morality and doing good things are not a prerequisite to come to Jesus. Truth is, you can be perfect on paper or a downright scumbag and still need Jesus. Romans 3:23 tells us that *all* of us have sinned—*all* of us fall short. , *"for all have sinned and fall short of the glory of God."* No sin is too much and no efforts are enough. But in order to get to Jesus, you have to accept what he did for you. You have to accept that the Son of God took on *your* sin. That he died for *you.* That he is no longer dead but sitting at the right hand of God. And that he loves you.

> *"But now the righteousness of God has been manifested apart from the law, although the Law and the Prophets bear witness to it—the righteousness of God through faith in Jesus Christ for all who believe. For there is no distinction: for all have sinned and fall short of the glory of God, and are justified by his grace as a gift, through the redemption that is in Christ Jesus, whom God put forward as a propitiation by his blood, to be received by faith."*
>
> Romans 3:21-25a (ESV)

Don't hesitate and don't worry about not being ready. You are ready. You don't have to know the Bible. That will come. You don't have to pray all fancy. But you do need to know what Jesus did for you. Then you need to confess. Confessing is such an ambiguous word, so let me make it simple. Confessing is basically self-awareness of your sin. It's saying out loud what your heart already knows. So, daughter, confess your sin. Talk to Jesus. There is freedom in bringing your sin to the light. Tell him all about it (as in right now). At Starbucks. In the car line. In your closet. Doesn't matter. Just confess and believe like Paul says in Romans 10:9:

> *...because, if you confess with your mouth that Jesus is Lord and believe in your heart that God raised him from the dead, you will be saved.*
>
> Romans 10:9 (ESV)

That's it! It's that simple. Now let that freedom in him, in knowing that you aren't a slave to sin, transform you. And just so you know, transformation won't happen in an instant. You won't all of a sudden stop sinning. In fact, you will forever have to walk away from sin; that's called repentance, and y'all it's hard. Like a moth to the flame, it's hard to 180 from our natural inclinations, but get excited because you are not condemned by your sin any longer. You are not defined by it. You are a new creation.

> *Therefore, if anyone is in Christ, he is a new creation. The old has passed away; behold, the new has come.*
>
> 2 Corinthians 5:17 (ESV)

Now, for your own sake, there's one more step: tell someone. Anyone. A pastor. That annoying coworker who always prays for you. Your mom. Me. Email me! Anyone. Everyone! Let someone walk with you.

Christians, let me repeat what I said in the introduction. You can't claim Jesus and park it in the complacency garage. You have to look different. You have to be different. You have to be moved. So moved that it overflows in your actions. So moved that it transforms you. I am so tired of people saying stuff like I love Jesus and I love Muslims and I love atheists and I love gays as if they wear some special badge of honor. Y'all, the last time I checked, all Christians should love all people. And if you don't love others recklessly like your Savior loves you then you really need to do some soul-searching. Because if you call yourself a Christian, you should love people so much that they want to know your Savior. Your love should literally take Jesus with you. You should love your coworker and your mother-in-law and your neighbor so much that nothing is more important than winning their soul to Jesus. Period. And if you don't, if you keep trying to be "relatable" so you don't scare people off, if you keep telling foul jokes to show people you're cool—if you keep taking shots with people at the bar, if you keep dropping the F bomb, you're not being real. You're confusing people. In fact, teaching someone about Jesus pointedly will not scare the lost! It's like my friend Charles says, "You can't scare someone from Christ who is already running from him." Man, I wish I could tattoo that on my forehead. Let me say that again in the tone in which I feel these words. **You cannot scare someone from Christ who is already running from him!**

Please don't hear condemnation from me. If anyone has bought into this faulty thinking, it's yours truly. But please, please, please, I beg you to let this concept puncture your soul the way it did mine. Please think about what it really means and how often we think like this. Think about the last time you wanted to share Jesus with a coworker or a friend. Or think about someone you want to share the gospel with now but have yet to do so. I mean really think about this as in stop what you're doing and reflect on your hesitancy in doing so. Reflect on your approach. Now, remember this. You can't mess it up. I don't care how inarticulate you are. I don't care how cool this person is and how uncool you are. It's not possible to thwart God's plan. You don't have the power. The book of Job says:

I know that you can do all things, and that no purpose of yours can be thwarted.

                                                              Job 42:2 (ESV)

So, before you tell yourself that you are afraid to tell someone about Jesus because you may mess it up, remember that you can't mess up the soul of someone the Holy Spirit is wooing.

I'll say it another way. If the Holy Spirit has put someone on your heart, he is already laying the groundwork; he's already working! You don't need to cuss a little. You don't need to drink too much. You don't need to laugh at sketchy jokes. You don't need to watch trash. You just have to be authentic. That's it. Not preachy. Not cool. Not a mute. Not overly spiritual. Not perfect. Just real. Because people want to see you, the real, struggling you, as you hold on to a hard relationship or walk through a hard time. They want to hear you speak words of life to them. They want your life to give them hope. They want you to tell them something different than the message they're currently receiving. And the crazy thing is that they probably don't even know what draws them to you. They have no idea that it's Jesus calling them. Don't silence his voice through you.

You cannot scare someone from Christ who is already running from him!

God is strategic. He does so much behind the scenes. To think we're the ones responsible for everything is kind of laughable. And pompous. The God of the universe, the God who created the very person you are scared to talk to, that is the God who will do all the work. He doesn't need you to be remarkable. He just needs you to be willing. I don't know about you, but that takes a huge weight off my chest. I don't have to be awesome. I don't have to know every Bible verse. I don't have to be perfect. I just have to let God be awesome. So, before you drink that third margarita with your coworker in an attempt to show them you're a fun Christian, remember that they want to see your consistent, reckless love for something bigger than yourself. They don't need another drinking buddy. They need Jesus.

I so badly want the lost to see me as being different in a complacent world. Shoot, I want other Christians to be motivated by my love for Jesus. Have you ever met someone like that? Maybe you know them from church or follow them on Instagram. They make you want to know their Jesus. Y'all, hold onto their words. Be around them as much as possible, because Jesus is calling you through them. And believe it or not, you are probably that for someone else already. Be the kind of girl who has people thinking, *I want what she has.* Don't be the girl who has people thinking Christians are a bunch of hypocritical idiots. We have enough of those already. People who make bogus statements like "I love Jesus but I cuss a little" are not the kind of people I'm telling you to be drawn to. Girl, no. These authors, bloggers, and friends may say some cool stuff that sounds empowering, even biblical in a way, but they are slightly off. Don't get me wrong, I think some of these women mean well, and they're motivating for sure, but if you join the party, if you start veering from Scripture, guess what? You're on the wide, inviting road to becoming frog legs.

These people make a big show of saying the right thing, but their hearts aren't in it. Because they act like they're worshiping me but don't mean it, I'm going to step in and shock them awake, astonish them, stand them on their ears.

Isaiah 29:13 (MSG)

14

Sister, trust him.

Sometimes I thank God for
unanswered prayers.
Garth Brooks

KIND OF FEEL blasphemous using the phrase "unanswered prayer" because it's obviously not a biblical statement. It also makes no sense. There's no such thing as an unanswered prayer. All prayers are answered. We just don't always like to hear "no" or "wait." But I really like the concept Garth is communicating in the opening quote here, so do me a favor: hear me out. Have an open mind and try your hardest to throw out the sound theology you may hold close to your heart.

You see, there was this guy I met in my young, young adulthood who literally made me swoon. I feel eighty years old using the word "swoon," but I literally have no other word to describe the feeling. You can roll your eyes all you want, but I know *you* know what I'm talking about. Think back to your first crush. Or when you met your husband. Remember the feeling? Anxiety. Light-headedness. Butterflies. You wanted to pass out, pee, and jump all at the same time.

I was barely out of high school at the time I met Mr. Swoon (lame, I know but I have to call him something). I serial-dated during this immature season of my young adulthood, but I dumped everyone after a couple of dates because they weren't him. Mr. Swoon was smart. He was a leader.

He knew exactly what he wanted out of life. And he was godly. I think. I mean, he had a ministry role, so in my mind at the time, that meant he had to be godly, right? And he was good looking. So good looking. He would be on stage talking about Jesus, and I was mesmerized. Y'all, he was everything I thought I wanted. I melted around the man. Literally, this man ruined me. I no longer had a vision for myself. I didn't have dreams. I was simply going to marry this man and go wherever he led me. Forget my dream of moving to a different part of the world. Or that strong, independent streak God burned into my soul as a little girl. That book God wanted me to write? Drop it. My passion to serve the poor? Whatever. I was going to be Mrs. Swoon and do whatever he did.

Then we dated. Kinda. We spent time together. And in that time he hurt me. Deeply. Not physically. But emotionally. Turns out Mr. Swoon wasn't so perfect, but I still pined for him. Oddly enough, in my pining (in a borderline pathetic kind of way) I grew more and more in love with Jesus. Being the immature, borderline pathetic girl I was at the time, I connected my faith journey with all of my prayers to marry Mr. Swoon. I mean, the guy was in ministry and I loved Jesus. I was the perfect match for his calling. Forget my calling. I didn't need one. I had his.

Then Mr. Swoon moved away. And whatever we were was no longer. And I was lost. I was forced to find myself. I was forced to make decisions. I was even forced to date the sloppy seconds that were left behind. But I still prayed Mr. Swoon would find his way back to me. Even after God confirmed in my heart that he was not the one, I just prayed harder. I held onto the parable of the persistent widow. You know how it goes. The woman in Luke 18 was basically so annoying that she got what she wanted:

> But because this widow won't quit badgering me, I'd better do something and see that she gets justice—otherwise I'm going to end up beaten black-and-blue by her pounding.
>
> Luke 18:5 (MSG)

That was me. The persistent widow, pounding God with my endless requests to be Mrs. Swoon. And God was the judge who could grant me that which I so desired. Only it didn't happen. God went radio silent. So, what did I do? I got angry. I remember telling God in one of my prayers that I didn't even want his will anymore. I wanted him to turn me loose and give me what I wanted: Mr. Swoon.

Who's with me here? Have you ever wanted something this badly? Have you ever still wanted it after knowing it wasn't good for you? Have you ever been so bold as to tell God you wanted your request more than his will? Have you ever secretly thought his will was lame? If you haven't, then I'm impressed. But if you have or if you know deep in your gut that this is you, take heart. The Lord did not strike me dead for my irreverent cries, and he won't take you out, either. I have four words to describe my relationship with Mr. Swoon: square peg, round hole. I know that now, but at the time, dang, it hurt. When I met Mr. Swoon, social media wasn't a thing, but as time passed, I was able to look into the life God gave him. He was married, of course. I was not. She was beautiful, of course.

And there I was, Miss Wild Card, trying to figure it all out. I felt like this stray white horse running free on the beach with nothing but the horizon in sight. And that terrified me. I'll save you the details, but let me tell you where Garth Brooks fits in to all this. Mr. Swoon is now married and has like five or six kids. I stopped looking him up after number four. Apparently, he lives in the country with his wife, who quit her high-profile job to raise his babies. They homeschool. They probably have chickens. I don't know. His life seems to have turned out wonderfully, but that's not the point of my story. The point in all this, the big dot deal is this: it was never about Mr. Swoon. What God was doing, what I was praying—it was never about him. It was always, I mean always, about God's glory and my good. Are you hearing me? Whatever you are asking him, wherever he appears to be quiet or saying no, has nothing to do with what you want so badly. Right smack in the middle of your desperate prayer. Right smack in the middle of your pain and pleas. Right smack in the middle of all that is his glory. Right smack in the middle of my immature prayer that asked the God of the universe to circumvent his perfect will for my petty request is an amazing Lord who refused to yield. A God who loved me too much to turn me loose on what I thought I wanted.

You see, my prayer did not go unanswered. Sister, your prayer is not going unanswered. Hardly. Those moments in the car when you're praying your guts out. The dates. The tears. The negative pregnancy tests. The bills. The doctor's visits. The yearnings of your soul. They are being collected in his perfect hands and held together with his amazing grace. The God of the universe. The God of Abraham, Isaac, and Jacob. The God of the Bible. That's the God who hears you. The Lord is holding the cards close to his chest, ready to make a play. In his time. In his way. He is setting up his move. And I assure you it will be a royal flush.

My royal flush has a name. Andrew. And, man, did God show off when he brought us together. Listen, by now you know that we struggled. It was very hard, so hard, but God transformed me because of that man. He also gave me a man who loves my fire. A man who would never want me to live on a farm with five or six kids. A man who loves dogs, not chickens. A man who knows my wiring and would never want me to quit my job. Or homeschool. Not that I'm knocking Mr. and Mrs. Swoon or their choice to birth a basketball team, homeschool, or even move to the country to do all those things. I have no doubt that Mrs. Swoon is exactly where God wants her to be. But had God given me over to *her* life, wow. I wouldn't even recognize the version of me who would want that.

You see, God didn't want me with Mr. Swoon for my good. God wanted to shape me and break me for his glory. God wanted my first years in marriage to suck so I could write about it, so I could help other women. God wanted me to deal with gossip and to struggle with my identity and the loss of a son so he could give me a story to tell. A book to write. While I was praying to marry some man I hardly knew, God saw all of that from his perfect, omnipotent view. Even when I prayed that stupid prayer in his name, there was no way he was going to let up knowing what he knew. He didn't turn his back on me for praying something so trivial either. Because guess what? It wasn't stupid and trivial at all. It was the longings of his daughter's heart.

Do you hear me? Your prayers to your heavenly Father are the pleas of his child's deepest longings. Know that when you approach the throne boldly—he cares about what you long for. And do just that: approach him boldly when you have the guts to actually pray for your longings. Like any parent, he may love you too much to say yes if it isn't best, but he longs to bless you. Just like you long to say yes to your children. Don't mistake his silence for not caring. But let's be real here. It's not that easy. Mr. Swoon is no one off. He is one of the many times I've wondered why God has gone radio silent. I bet half the people reading this right now are struggling with a seemingly unanswered prayer. Wanting a husband.

Weight issues. Infertility. A bad job. Health problems. Wanting someone you love to change. We all want something. We all have that plea waiting to be answered. Maybe, like me, you want to be rescued from something. Maybe you think this one thing will make everything else okay.

Hear me loud and clear when I say this: Apart from the prayer to have Christ take over your soul, no answer to any prayer will save you. No man. No baby. No job. No amount of money. Why? Because we have a Savior. Mr. Swoon was not my Savior. Your daddy is not your Savior. Your husband is not your Savior. Your baby, your perfect rainbow baby, guess what? Not your Savior. All that extra cash from a better job or promotion? Not your Savior. A cure to cancer or your autoimmune disease? Again, not your Savior. I don't care what it is, the answer remains the same: not your Savior. Sister, if God has not answered some prayer of yours yet, no matter how sad, mad, or tired you are, trust his sovereignty. If he seems to be giving you the dreaded "wait" hand, that's not a "Bye Felicia," and it's certainly not an unanswered prayer. There's no such thing. Garth Brooks: There is no such thing. And if you're anything like the persistent widow, praying fervently for something that seems to make complete sense to you, feeling like you're talking to thin air, know this: God isn't ignoring you. He isn't mad at you or holding out on you because of some sin in your past. No way. He is collecting your deep gut cries, your longings, your private laments, and he's setting up his next play. Because, y'all, God is amazing at poker.

> *Those moments in the car when you're praying*
> *your guts out. . . . The yearnings of your soul.*
> *They are being collected in his perfect hands and*
> *held together with his amazing grace. . . .*
>
> *The Lord is holding the cards close to his chest,*
> *ready to make a play. In his time. In his way. He is*
> *setting up his move.*

My husband and I celebrated our ten-year anniversary in 2019, and I want to share with you what I posted on social media:

Ten years. Ten years! I do not say this lightly. I say this as honestly and straightforward as I can: We shouldn't be here. We should have divorced years ago. Let me rephrase that. I wanted to be divorced years ago. But God. That's one of my favorite sayings. But God. But God in his full grace chose to work on my selfish heart full of unrealistic expectations. But God in his full grace chose to save the marriage of two sinful people and make it something beautiful. I am no walk in the park. My husband is long-suffering and loyal. He extends so much grace. Praise God for the people who have poured into us over the years and pointed us back to Jesus and to each other when times were tough. People refer to miracles when someone's PET scan comes back clean. Or when they walk away from a car wreck untouched. What people don't realize is the miracle it takes in changing the hearts of two stubborn, sinful people. You just don't see that very often. My marriage is a miracle. I am so, so, so grateful for God's redemption. I'm not sure why he chose to redeem my marriage and not someone else's, but I'll spend all my days singing his praises in gratitude. As I reflect on the last years, I have to admit that I do not have the life I always thought I'd have. I have a life better than I could've ever imagined or prayed for.

I would not trade one day before meeting Andrew. I would not trade one ounce of the process. I would not take away the pain, the mistakes, the waiting, the bad dates. None of it. And I most certainly would not choose Mr. Swoon. Trust God, y'all. Trust him with your questions, your requests, your heart. Trust God. Because, listen, had I married Mr. Swoon, had it all fallen into place like I wanted way back when, I would not be writing this. I wouldn't be sitting at my marker-stained kitchen table, drinking my tenth cup of coffee, and telling my story while my kids are at school. I wouldn't have the pleasure of working as a social worker in my hometown. I wouldn't have three babies who have all seemed to inherit my fire and their daddy's smarts. I wouldn't have Henry waiting for me in heaven. I'd be on a farm. I'd be homeschooling. I'd be running after my five or six babies. I'd probably have chickens too. And while that may be God's plan for Mrs. Swoon, that, my friends, was never my story.

You ask and do not receive, because you ask wrongly, to spend it on your passions.

James 4:3 (ESV)

15

Sister, there is no "them."

*It's all right to tell a man to lift himself by
his own bootstraps, but it is cruel jest to
say to a bootless man that he ought to lift
himself by his own bootstraps.*
Martin Luther King Jr.

I GREW UP PRETTY privileged. It has taken me a long time to realize
this and an even longer time to admit it out loud, but there it is. I lived
in a nice home. At sixteen I had my own car. Going to the college of my
choice was never an issue. Basically, I never wanted for a thing. Growing
up, everyone around me was fairly well off too. Everyone around me
had money. Everyone around me wanted for nothing as well. Sadly, this
shaped me, and I assumed this was the norm. My parents taught me to
love Jesus and exposed me to poverty and other social issues to help me
learn compassion and understanding, but even so, my lens was pretty
narrow based on my environment. After college, however, I started
seeing things differently. I tried to understand matters of social justice
the best I could, but I'll admit that I still saw everything through my lens.
I still didn't understand how the poor couldn't just make better decisions.
"Why can't 'they' read a Dave Ramsey book like the rest of us?" I couldn't
understand why people would buy cigarettes and not their medications.

I couldn't wrap my head around the young mom having her fifth kid at twenty-two.

Tell me I'm not the only one who is guilty of thinking like this. Tell me you, too, have wondered why people can't just get a job and stop being homeless. Tell me you, too, have wondered why everyone can't just go to college and stop depending on the government. Feel free to insert your own expectations of the poor here. Not just the poor in riches. I'm talking about the poor in spirit as well. The least of these. The marginalized. The underdog, if you will. So, take a minute and consider your own prejudices. Your own faulty thinking. Opinions based on your personal experiences and seen through your limited perspective—not the Lord's. Whoever says ignorance is bliss was spot on. Life was actually easier for me when I was oblivious to the rest of the world. I didn't hurt like I do now.

Part of me wishes I never knew what I've learned since becoming a social worker. I would erase the look on my patient Bob's face as he explains that he has lost forty pounds because he can't get to food. That kind of stuff I expect somewhere else, but not in America. Not in my backyard. "Why can't Bob just go to a local food bank?" you ask. Great question. I asked the same one myself. He doesn't have transportation. "Can't you take the bus? Or walk? Or call Meals on Wheels or something?" Again, great questions. In fact, I asked Bob all of these questions. Turns out if you live in a small town, you don't have those options. "What about food stamps?" you might be thinking. "Surely the man can get food stamps. If this man were truly poor, surely tax dollars can help him." Sadly, these were my thoughts as well. These were my exact words before I stopped talking and listened to this man's story.

Bob wasn't raised in a safe, comfortable, two-parent household. Bob wasn't raised by educated, well-meaning parents. Bob was actually raised by a pretty broken mother, who unfortunately was unable to break the cycle of addiction and neglect. Bob started off with a shaky foundation, but he was determined to be different. He decided he would work hard and never walk down the path of his parents. He did well in school. He stayed away from alcohol and drugs. He even started working at the age of fifteen. Then at the age of thirty, he was fired when he hurt his shoulder and couldn't work for a few days. Bob did what he could to survive. He couldn't make ends meet, so he decided to weather the pain and sell his pain meds so he could buy food. Only he sold them to the wrong guy and got arrested. And now he's marked as a felon.

So again, I ask you the million-dollar question: why can't Bob just get food stamps like every other poor person in America? I'll tell you why. Because Bob had a felony on his record when he applied, he was excluded from the food stamp program. And other benefits. And most jobs. Some of these laws have changed over the last decade, but at the time, this young man, who tried so hard to break the poverty cycle, couldn't. He just couldn't. And because of that he couldn't get the medication he needed for his genetic heart condition.

Let's change perspectives for a second so you can feel the full weight of this. Imagine Bob grew up in the suburbs. Imagine Bob got busted selling his mother's pain killers or imagine he got a DUI on the way home from his senior prom. Do you know how many kids I grew up with who have this woven into their story? Who have had multiple DUIs on their record and yet still hold CEO jobs? You see, Bob's daddy doesn't know a lawyer. Or a judge. Or a cop. He can't pick himself up by his bootstraps. The man doesn't even have boots.

But what about the poor in spirit? What about those ostracized by society due to their appearance or their lifestyle? What about my twenty-six-year old patient who sent me pictures of herself before her house caught fire several years ago. The pictures she labeled "When I Used to Be Beautiful." Turns out nobody wants to befriend a burn victim with a different looking face. I literally get sick to my stomach as I replay the words of a Christian friend who told me, "I think it's time to move. There are too many Black people in my neighborhood. I feel unsafe." Or the man I overheard at church saying he was looking for a reason to fire a gay employee because it doesn't look very Christian to have him on his payroll. I wanted to throw a Bible in this man's face. I wanted to plead for my Christian friend to read any one of the four Gospels, because this does not represent the Jesus I know. I wanted to remind this sweet girl that the God who created her doesn't care what her face looks like. To him, she is beautiful. The Jesus I know says, "Come as you are." The Jesus I know touched the leper. He healed the hemorrhaging woman. He ate with sinners. He asked Zacchaeus if he could come over and break bread with him.

Fast-forward to the twenty-first century. Y'all, I believe with every fiber in my being that Jesus here today would allow a gay man to work for him, would ask the man into his home. He would absolutely serve him his best. Shame on anyone for being afraid to be in the company of sinners. For thinking appearances are what wins souls. Shame on my Christian friend for being afraid of her neighbors because of the color of their skin. For thinking another neighbor would somehow be less of a threat for being white. Shame on me for thinking a poor mother can easily break the cycle of generational poverty by reading a Dave Ramsey book. Shame on Bob's local church for not knowing the story of the very people in their small community. Shame on me for turning my face for so long. Do you know how many people I've judged through my narrow lens? So many things we "Christians" think are true about the poor and the outcasts of society are not words uttered by Jesus. They are the antithesis of everything he stands for. They are words shaped by our sheltered, little worlds. They are actions shaped by our upbringing and the circles we keep. And these toxic words, these toxic actions, they are damaging. Literally, we are repelling Jesus to those who need him most. In Mark 2, Jesus and his disciples entered the home of a tax collector and ate with a bunch of outlaws. When the Pharisees saw him eating with sinners, they questioned his behavior. His response should be our response.

> When Jesus heard this, he told them, "Healthy people don't need a doctor—sick people do. I have come to call not those who think they are righteous, but those who know they are sinners.
>
> Mark 2:17 (NLT)

Y'all, Jesus has come for the sinners. For you. For me. For Bob. For your three-times divorced cousin. For your gay brother. For your mean coworker. That's why he came. That's why he died.

It would be so much easier to live in ignorance. To go about living in my safe, little corner where my biggest problem is affording a trip to Disney World or my kid's braces. To stay in my affluent neighborhood reading Christian books and just gaining knowledge. Going to Bible study with other people who look and think like me. Donating my scraps to the poor while selling my "nicer" things so I can buy more stuff I don't need. Y'all, staying clear of the messy lives around us is the easy path. Not knowing keeps us from having to change our attitudes, and to respond. Not knowing keeps us from having to love difficult people. Not knowing, sisters, makes us Pharisees.

The Bible has hundreds of references regarding the poor, both monetarily and in spirit. Not one of them, not a single one of these verses asks that you merely pray about throwing action toward the poor. Serving the poor isn't a ministry. It's not a spiritual gift. It's an overflow of our love for Jesus. In fact, 1 John 3:17 says:

> *If someone has enough money to live well and sees a brother or sister in need but shows no compassion—how can God's love be in that person?*
>
> 1 John 3:17 (NLT)

Staying clear of the messy lives around us is the easy path. Not knowing keeps us from having to change our attitudes, and to respond.

Not knowing keeps us from having to love difficult people. Not knowing, sisters, makes us Pharisees.

You can't love God and not love *all* of his people. It's just not possible. We have to be willing to ditch the prosperity mentality and love like Jesus. We have to shift our lens and expectations of others and start serving. No, we have to start posturing ourselves beneath people regardless of socioeconomic status. We have to love without judgment. Preaching that one can change their circumstances with enough hard work and prayer is ignorant and cruel to someone like my patient Bob. Imagine his face as you tell him that if he would just go to church or pray more, he, too, could have the awesome life you have. I don't say this lightly because this used to be my MO. This was my MO for so long. I used to wonder why poor people couldn't just work harder. Why mentally ill people couldn't just take their meds or see a therapist. Why unhealthy people couldn't just diet and exercise and so on and so on. That is, until I did everything "right," did all the things, and still bore a dead child. All the while attending church, keeping to the law, and working hard. All the while taking my prenatal vitamins. All the while praying for this child.

So, while it's tempting to tell you that if you do the work, you will overcome all your issues this side of glory, I can't do that. Life will still be hard—but don't miss my point. For many of us it is harder. So, who are we to tell a poor man or woman created in God's image who has no support, and perhaps medical and/or mental health issues, that if they work hard, then they, too, can live the American dream? Health, wealth, and the pursuit of happiness is within all our grasps, right? Wrong. Not everyone gets that option. Not everyone has a pair of boots.

This "us" and "them" attitude is unbiblical, and I guarantee it makes Jesus want to hurl. I don't care who you are, we all have a prejudice in some capacity and may I be so bold as to ask you to self-reflect on yours. Do you think everyone is capable of picking themselves up by their bootstraps? Do you think you are superior because you have money? Are you part of the white flight exodus? Do you distrust Blacks? Latinos? How about Muslims? Do you roll your eyes when you see a young mother with five kids at the grocery store using food stamps? The only way you can stop this mentality is by leaning into it and owning up to your own bias. It may be uncomfortable, but ask yourself if you would be upset if your child's best friend was from a different culture or a lower economic status. Ask yourself if you would ever ask a gay couple to have dinner in your home. Do you think poor people choose to stay poor? I'll tell you one thing for sure: I don't want my kids to see skin color or money. I want them to see souls. I don't want them to know if we are rich or poor. I want their security to be found in Jesus.

Listen to me. You can say you love Jesus all day long, but if you think that someone can just pull themselves up by their bootstraps, you have some praying to do. You're not a bad person, you just need to change this way of thinking. And, sister, you cannot change, we cannot change, by staying in our comfort zone. We have to expose ourselves. We have to take a bath in the words of Jesus because he loves us so well. One of my favorite stories in all of Scripture is the woman at the well in John 4. It's beauty. It's grace. It's the heart of Jesus. Allow me to paraphrase this love story. Jesus cuts through Samaria to make his route shorter. He's tired and thirsty because the Middle East is, well, dry and hot as fire. On his shortcut, he encounters a woman. Jesus, being unconventional, breaks tradition and talks to her. He asks her to get him a drink. There are so many things wrong with this, but the part I want you to really understand is that the woman he is speaking to in public was looked upon as a whore. This woman had five husbands and was living with a man she wasn't married to. This was not the twenty-first century where divorce and cohabitation were accepted by the culture. This was abnormal and scandalous for that era. Naturally, this made her an outcast to society, but here's the cool part. Jesus did not give it a second thought. He loved her. He challenged her. He revealed himself to her. An outcast. A promiscuous woman. A woman labeled a whore to most but lovely to him. And guess what? She left that encounter *changed.*

Nowhere in Scripture does Jesus ask anyone to "try harder." Never does he assume someone is not worth loving. No one is unreachable. In fact, the only group he rebukes are the pompous elite who condemn the very people he came to save. Y'all, we have to stop the lecturing and the eye rolling and the condemning. We have to stop thinking that our three-thousand-square-foot homes are the norm and widen our view of this messy, fallen world. We have to stop assuming everyone has the same opportunities we do. Instead, we need to love the way Jesus loved the woman at the well. We need to eat with sinners like he did with the tax collectors and their friends. We need to love the unlovable. We need to reach the unreachable. And the only way to do that is through the overflow of his love in us. Love God. Love people. That, my friend, sums it up.

So now I am giving you a new commandment: Love each other. Just as I have loved you, you should love each other.

John 13:34 (NLT)

16

Sister, back off.

Be not angry that you cannot make others
as you wish them to be, since you cannot
make yourself as you wish yourself to be.
Thomas à Kempis, The Imitation of Christ

READ SOMEWHERE THAT when you get married, a man wants
nothing more than his wife to stay the same, while women start trying
to change a man the moment they say, "I do." This couldn't have been
truer for me. When I started dating Andrew, I was pretty much a rock
star. Well, at least he thought so. I was Sporty Spice and went to every
sporting event you can name. We stayed up late. We heard live bands
and had happy hour. I wore nice clothes that showed off my curves. You
hardly saw me without makeup. And I never, I mean absolutely never,
farted in front of my man. In fact, I never even discussed going number
two. I was proper. I was arm candy. I was always down for a good time.

Then we got married. And I got constipated on the honeymoon. What
can I say, my bowels were shy in Jamaica. My going number two was the
theme of the entire trip. Then it spilled over into our real life. I tested
the waters with no makeup. He didn't say anything, so unless I was at
work, I was all natural. And sports? Are you kidding me? That was just
something I tolerated in order to be with my guy. I had him now. Did he
really think I was going to spend every night watching ESPN? I traded

my stilettos for flip-flops. I'm pretty sure I never wore a bra. And tight clothes? They were a thing of the past. Happy hour became a Route 44 Diet Coke from Sonic, and I preferred to spend my nights at home rather than hear live music.

My husband said nothing. I mean, I'm sure he had thoughts of my returning to "Cool Kim," but he rolled with it. I, on the other hand, tried to change him the day I became a Dafferner. Not that he needed to change. I just tried to mold him into who I thought God wanted him to be—who *I* thought he should be.

"You really need to be in a Bible study."

"Do you really need another beer?"

"You shouldn't golf so much. It's selfish."

"You need to make more money."

Who talks this way to a person? Tell me I'm not the only self-righteous brat with a critical tongue. Tell me I'm not the only jerk who looks at someone and tells them they need to be more, to be better, all the while struggling with my own self-esteem. I used to beg God to change Andrew. I prayed for his success, that he would love Jesus more, that he wouldn't be so selfish. I prayed that he would love *me* more. That he would join *my* world. That he would shower me with attention and affection—but leave me alone when I wanted him to, of course. I begged God to change him the way Paul was changed on the road to Damascus. I prayed that there would be this "aha" moment and *poof* he would be this perfect soap opera man. But God didn't see it my way. In fact, he made it very clear to me that Andrew wasn't the problem. *I was justifying my own behavior by focusing on his.*

I feel like a lot of us, me included, make up levels of sin. We think our issue with watching Netflix trash in no way compares to our husband's drinking problem, friend's porn addiction, or coworker's potty mouth. We think that stalking an ex on social media in no way compares to a full-on affair. Basically, we compare our sins, and in that comparison, the litmus test is no longer the Bible's truth, but our flawed humanity. While there are different consequences for different actions, excusing your behavior by condemning someone else's is hypocritical at best. Self-justification has no place in the kingdom. Accepting God's grace for your own sin yet not pouring it out on someone else is not the way of Jesus.

Truth is, the cross is enough to cover my behavior—and yours. His grace is abounding, and all sin is covered for those willing to nail it to the cross.

To those of you who nag your husbands . . .

To those of you who helicopter your kids . . .

To those of you who micromanage your employees . . .

To those of you who spew ugly comments all over social media . . .

> **Accepting God's grace for your own sin yet not pouring it out on someone else is not the way of Jesus.**

If any of these signs of self-justification apply to you, tell me, how's it going? I'm being serious. Is your controlling, judgmental behavior changing anyone? I'm not asking if it's spurring action. Most people will do whatever it takes to get their biggest critic to shut up. But have you changed any hearts? Have you inspired anyone to want to transform from the inside out? If you're nagging, controlling, manipulating, or firing on social media, my guess is no. For real, do you know a single soul who longed to know Jesus because a self-righteous Christian pointed out their sin? Do you know *anyone* who longed to understand their own prejudices after being attacked on social media? Have you ever met anyone who was *more* able to hear the Holy Spirit because their mom controlled their every move during childhood? Y'all, I don't know a husband on the planet who has changed for the better because his wife told him he doesn't work hard enough or that he's too fat or that he's a horrible spiritual leader—or father. Do you? Writing this makes my insides crawl because I still catch myself justifying my own sins—forgetting that Jesus died on the same cross for all of us, for somehow thinking his grace was enough for my sins but not someone else's.

So how do we fix this? How do we stop trying to change everyone around us? How do we stop comparing our sins to others? It's very simple. We change ourselves. We stay in our own lane. We change what we can, which is within us, and accept that everything beyond that is out of our control. We release everyone else to God. I believe the folks at

Alcoholics Anonymous have it right when they daily repeat the serenity prayer of St. Francis of Assisi:

> *God, grant us the serenity to accept the things we cannot change, the courage to change the things we can, and the wisdom to know the difference.*

Accept the things we cannot change. Your child with special needs. Your parents. Your chronic illness. Your husband's job. Other people's choices or attitudes. You can't change any of these things, do you hear me? You have no power over these things. Pray like a mad woman. Pray for a miracle. Pray for healing. Pray for change. But also come to terms with them. I beg you. Freedom is on the other side of acceptance.

Change the things we can. Your diet. Your boundaries. Your reactions to people. Your compliance with medication for your illness. Your job. Your friends. The order in your home. These are just a few of the things you *can* change. Change *them*. No excuses. You hold the power. You can fix so much more than you think you can. Stop whining. Stop crying. Stop making excuses. Stop eating cookies and wallowing. Fix them. I beg you. Freedom is on the other side of changing what you can.

The wisdom to know the difference. This is the hard part. This is the part that requires prayer. And friends. Sometimes we need to go to a trusted pastor or spiritual leader. Sometimes we may even need professional help. Listen, sometimes we need help knowing what we need to change and what we need to accept. Sometimes we are so deep in our stories that we can pray like crazy but still lack an objective point of view. Seek the guidance you need to know the difference. I've sought help from friends, pastors, trusted leaders, and, yes, professionals. There is no shame in any of it. Knowing what you can change, what you should change, versus knowing what you need to accept matters. Deciphering between the two makes all the difference. Because there is a difference— and there is power in *knowing* the difference.

There is so much life in the words of St. Francis. I know it's scary letting go of the need to intervene and control. *I know.* I mean, what if your spouse thinks you're condoning his behavior because you stop trying to change him? What if your kids think you're cool with them exploring other religions when you stop beating them over the head with your Bible? What if people think your peaceful response means you're giving up?

Here's the part where I remind you of something you already know. You have no power over other people. None. Zero. Zilch. You need to tell yourself this every single day. While you're at it, remind yourself that you are literally wasting your time. While your heart is in the right place, it's actually counterproductive. All you're doing is pushing people away from you and from Jesus. Your nagging is actually a form of unbelief. You are not trusting Jesus to do what he's best at: saving the people he loves. Sister, there's a God out there who loves your children more than you do. A God who wants your husband to be godly. A God who wants the best for you. A God who wants your children to love him. And guess what? You have access to him. You have the insane privilege to plea to him day in and day out. In fact, he delights in it. He wants you to ask him for hard things. He wants to show you that he is capable of changing the seemingly impossible.

Here's where you have all the power. You have the power to take it to him. The people who hurt you. The people you want to change. Beg the Holy Spirit to get loud in their hearts. Beg your Father to crank up the volume in your children's ears. Beg the Lord to convict your husband's unrepentant heart. Then do me a favor. Back the heck up and let him work. I mean it. God doesn't need you to micromanage the people he created. He delights to work in their lives. What more could he want then to have the souls of your children and your husband? He wants you to want *that*, pray for it, and believe him for it. Trust the same Holy Spirit who wooed you. Trust that still small voice to pull your babies in. Trust that he will speak to your man's heart—then shut up. I'm serious. Shut your mouth. The Holy Spirit can't convict your husband if you're talking over him.

Random question, but have you ever planted flowers? I don't have much of a green thumb, but I've put flowers in a pot. That's easy. My four-year-old daughter can do that. In fact, she helped me do it the other day. We took her purple flowers out of their plastic seeding container and put them in a pot with the intention of letting nature do its thing. Just before I put it on the front porch, my husband intervened. He told me that, without a little help, Sydney's flowers would die—and he wasn't about to let his baby girl's flowers die. With my permission, my

Boy Scout husband emptied the pot and added new soil. Fresh soil. He added an enhancer to the dirt. Then he put the pot in the perfect spot where the flowers would get the perfect sun-shade combo. He explained to our daughter that nature is powerful and glorious, but that we have the power to help the process. We need to water our flowers. We need to tend to them daily because the right amount of water and sun will prime them to be their absolute best. Do you see where I'm going with this?

You can throw dirt in a pot and hope for the best, just like you can throw words and control at your loved ones and hope for the best. You may get a few action changes here and there, but it's not sustainable. But love and encouragement? Now, that's fertile soil. It evokes growth and change. It's the primer for the best possible outcome. At the risk of sounding like a cheese ball, let me say that you can be fertile soil for your children. You can be the soil enhancer for your husband. You can tend to him with the perfect amount of sun and shade. You can water him just enough. You can create the best environment possible and then let God do his thing. That, my friends, is how we change others. We give them the best opportunity to hear God. We give them the foundation they need to bloom. Does this mean you coddle poor behavior? Absolutely not. Can you still call people out on their dysfunction? One hundred percent yes, but not with criticism. Gently. Kindly. Lovingly. With their best in mind, yes, we should point our people to Jesus. But when we call people out, we should be *for* them. For God's best for them—not for what we think they should be, and definitely not with ourselves and expectations in mind.

I know, this is hard stuff. It's so easy to Monday morning quarterback other people's lives. It's so easy to look at someone and wonder why they are doing that one destructive thing "again." Smoking. Overeating. Drugs. Spending. Judging. Yet we forget how difficult it is to change ourselves. It feels unnatural, really. I mean, I can't even stay on a thirty-day no-sugar diet without cheating. A workout challenge I paid for? Nope. But somehow I find it okay to micromanage how often my husband goes to Bible study. That's insane. And I hope to Jesus that you know what I'm talking about. Tell me you understand what I'm talking about here. Tell me how easy it is for you to see the speck in someone's eye and miss the log in your own. I don't know about you, but I want to recover from self-justification. I want to want what God wants. I want to change myself while I pray for others. I want to trust God with what he does best: change the heart of people.

Isn't it astounding the way we give ourselves the grace to be human, yet we can't seem to dig deep and give others the same compassion? We hold out our hands and accept his will and the sanctification process. In fact, we have come to terms with imperfect progress in ourselves. Yet our spouse or children show imperfection of any kind, and we are all over it with judgment.

"I can't believe he is still struggling with that same sin."

"I can't believe she acts like that."

"I can't believe they live that way."

Meanwhile, we still struggle with our own issues time and time again.

Y'all, we have to trust that the Holy Spirit is behind us. That he will do the work. That he is for our good. We have to trust his process. We have to trust that he will change our babies, our husbands, and us. We have to trust that his image is far greater than our created image. Do you really want your creation over what the God of the Universe created? It's like choosing art from Hobby Lobby instead of a Vincent van Gogh.

Three things will last forever—faith, hope, and love—and the greatest of these is love.

1 Corinthians 13:13 (NLT)

17

Sisters, wake up!

God has not redeemed you to dwell in a
Christian bubble; he has redeemed you to
spread the Christian gospel.
David Platt

THERE ARE THREE things in life that make me want to barf. First, bananas. Seriously, just talking about them has me gagging. They're mushy. They smell bad. Gross. Just gross. Snot is a close second. I don't mind my kids' snot for some reason, but if I see even a little dribble coming out of someone else's nose, I throw up in my mouth. The last thing, y'all, the last thing that makes me want to barf is something more serious. The thing in life that makes me want to throw things, cry, and barf all at the same time? Christians who hide in church. I didn't say Christians who *go* to church. I also didn't say *Christians* in general. But I did use the word "hide" because so many of us are hiding behind the Bible or activity or right in the midst of our church community.

So often we keep ourselves and our children "protected" in the walls of the church and fail to *be* the church in our everyday lives. We go to Bible study after Bible study, yet we never put ourselves in an environment that actually needs to hear what we've learned. Don't get me wrong, I love a good Wednesday night church dinner. And Sunday church. And life group. And Bible study. I also love me some vacation Bible school and youth retreats. Those are good things—*great* things. But we sometimes keep ourselves so busy with all of the "Christian" things that we miss the opportunity on the soccer field. Or at work. Or in our neighborhood. Or how about the lady at the grocery store? Or the gas station? I know I miss these opportunities. I love to stay in my bubble of like-minded folks. It's easier. It's safe and comfortable. But, listen, it's wrong—and it is not at all the way Jesus lived.

Before I continue, I have to stop and reiterate that church attendance is a must. As in, in-person church. Where you see faces. This is where you get fuel. This is where you are equipped. Reading the Bible? That's also a must. You have to read and know your Bible. Doing life with people in your church? Yes! This is where you find your tribe. This is your accountability. But the point of going to church, knowing the Bible, and being with other believers is not to bubble you from the world. It isn't to stay comfortable with people like you. It isn't a checklist of things you do because it's expected or safe. No, girl. It's to "go and tell." It's to be stirred and motivated to unleash his presence on the world. For various reasons, we get caught up in the *things* of God but not in God himself. We go through the motions of being a Christian without having a heart for the things we do.

We are a generation of free thinkers. People have never felt more open to question the world around them. To rebel against their upbringing. To search for answers. To buck cultural norms. And do you know where Christians should be? Not hiding in church. Not hiding at home reading the Bible. Nope. We need to be right in the middle of those questions. We need to be in people's homes. We need to be at happy hour building relationships with our questioning coworkers. We need to be asking our neighbors into *our* homes. Y'all, we need to be sharing the gospel with anyone willing to listen. What I love most about free thinkers is how real they are. Their authenticity is astounding and, oh my stars, it's a surefire pathway to talk about Jesus. Don't know how to respond to some of those free-thinking statements? Here are some ways to keep the conversation going:

"You hate God? You hate church? Tell me what happened."
"You think Christians are hypocrites? What does being a Christian mean to you?"

"You had an abortion? That must have been hard. How are you
doing?"
"You cheated on your spouse? How did things get to that point?"
"You say you are a functioning alcoholic. Tell me why you drink."
"You think you might be gay. Talk me through it."

Let's go there. Let's take time to hear these stories. Let's hear how
people got to this place because behind all these stories is pain. And
while pain sucks, that very hole is the exact backdrop where people meet
a Savior. Your Savior. And I don't know about you, but I want them to
know him so badly. That's the reason he created us. That's why he came
to this earth. And, Christian, that's why he died for us. Don't keep him
so close to your vest.

But don't miss this next part. We have to physically take Jesus to
people. They're not going to come to us, and we can't do that hiding
in our safe little community. We can't do that behind the walls of our
church. We can't engage with people who need Jesus if we're at Bible
study every night. Those are great places to fuel up and vital places for
restoration; in fact, you can't share the gospel unless you know the Word
of God. However, there comes a point where we have to "go." We can't
selfishly hold the gospel close to our chests and hope for the best. We are
called, no, we are *commanded* to share this life-changing news with our
neighbors. Psalm 96 says,

Take the news of his glory to the lost, news of his wonders to one and
all!

Psalm 96:3 (MSG)

Luke 19:1–10 tells the story of a tax collector named Zacchaeus. I
learned this story when I was a toddler, but it never occurred to me how
impactful it would be to my life today. For those of you who don't know
this story or are a little rusty, allow me to refresh your memory. Back in
Jesus' day, tax collectors were frowned upon. They were reviled the way
we hate scammers who rip off old people's social security checks. Zacchaeus was a rich tax collector who happened to be very short. He was so
short, in fact, that when Jesus came to town, Zacchaeus climbed a tree to
see him. I'm not exactly sure why he wanted to see Jesus. Perhaps he was

curious to see what all the hype was about. Or maybe, just maybe, God was already wooing him, and he just had to lay eyes on Jesus. Knowing God, the latter is likely true. When Jesus passed Zacchaeus, he literally stopped in his tracks and told him to get out of the tree. Can you imagine? You're trying to be inconspicuous. You're watching from a distance and you're called out. I'm sure Zacchaeus was mortified and three shades of red as he climbed down the tree. Imagine the stares he got when Jesus tells him that he's coming over.

I love the way Jesus breaks all the rules. He literally takes cultural norms and crushes them. We live in a pretty modern culture, so Jesus having lunch with Zacchaeus doesn't seem like a big deal, but I assure you that this was a major faux pas for that era. This is the equivalent of the pope having dinner with Hugh Hefner at the Playboy Mansion. Jesus lived missionally and intentionally, so he didn't care one iota about cultural acceptance. He not only welcomed sinners like Zacchaeus, but he pursued them. I love The Message version of the Pharisees' response to Jesus' invite in Luke 19:7: *"What business does he have getting cozy with this crook?"* Ha! Jesus didn't care what these Pharisees thought of him. He was pursuing a lost man no matter the cost. The story ends with Zacchaeus being a changed man and Jesus saying, *"For the Son of Man came to find and restore the lost"* (Luke 19:10b MSG). Talk about redemption!

Christians, we have the bonus of living in a generation that values authenticity, a culture where it's okay to have an opinion and speak up. Look at the marriage equality movement. These advocates refused to be quiet, and laws have been changed. The definition of a woman is being redefined. Transgender bathrooms are happening. Christians, we have to speak up! Other groups are driving their agendas forward and what are we doing? We are hiding in church and keeping our heads in our Bibles. We pray yet we do nothing radical. We are literally quarantining ourselves from the very people who need to hear about Jesus. The woman who aborted her child? The world is telling her it's okay, that it's just a clump of cells, that it's her body, her choice. Christians, where are we? This woman needs peace. This woman needs forgiveness. She needs the radical love of Jesus, much like the love He showed to the woman at the well. She doesn't need us to condone her decision. In fact, I'm tired of Christians being silent because they're scared they will be labeled judgmental. That's a cop out. You and I both know you can speak against sin and injustice and still love the mess out of someone. Jesus did it all the time. In fact, loving someone well leads them to the cross. Don't buy into this intolerance agenda. Sister, don't you dare get roped into silence.

Or what about the little boy who struggles with his pronoun? Or the woman who is unhappy and wants out of her marriage? Guess who is getting their message out—people who are not interested in preserving God's word, that's who. In fact, most of the people speaking up dismiss God's word altogether. They talk a lot about love, and define it by saying, "you do you," and "God made you just the way you are." When pressed on hard issues like abortion they use words like "women's reproductive rights." When asked if homosexual marriage is Biblical, they argue "love is love." Love, love, love. "All you need is love." "God is the God of love." True, God is absolutely the God of love, but here's my question. Does love mean God affirms all your decisions, or that we affirm everyone else's decisions? Is that what we are saying love is? Is love pushing someone toward temporary happiness? Is love encouraging someone to "live life to the fullest"? Because if that's your definition of love, then I get it. I'm tracking with you one hundred percent. But don't claim that this is the message of Christ, because it's not. Anyone can open their Bible and see that it's not.

Before I continue, let me clarify something very important. I'm talking to Christians here. I don't expect someone who doesn't know Jesus yet to live according to the Bible. I'm speaking directly to Christians who are spewing bad theology to their co-workers or affirming worldly agendas by their silence. I'm speaking to Christians who have created a god in their own image by telling the world about a god who isn't the God of the Bible. To you, Christians, I'm sorry (but I'm not sorry) to say this: Love is caring about someone's soul, not affirming their destructive decisions. You will never convince me love is anything but leading someone to the cross. Any other message is false. Here's the problem with this "everything's ok" theology: it misrepresents the Lord completely. It creates this "hippie" Jesus who loves everyone just as they are (true) but tells people they should stay the way they are (not true). God is the God of transformation, not stagnation. God loves you, yes, but He wants to restore you. He is for your peace, not your convenience. He is for your holiness, not your happiness.

Sister, stay away from those who bless what God curses and curse what God blesses. Stay away from those who tell you what you *want* to hear, not what you *need* to hear. Stay away from anyone who does not believe in the inerrancy of Scripture. I understand you will be in the minority. I understand you will be labeled judgy and intolerant, but I'll tell you what I tell my kids. Just because someone says something does not make it true. Let me go further with this. You and I will stand before God one day. The chances of this are one hundred percent. Do you really want to give the crowd what they want to hear, or do you want to please the God of the universe? Because here's the deal. The god you create in our own image, He ain't God. The god who is "YOLO" and for "you doing you," is not the God of the Bible. Sadly, these self-centered agendas lead to destruction.

Sister, God is the God who is after your soul. He is the God who wants you to have peace, not false comfort. He is the God who wants what is holy, and pure, and just. This may mean that you get cancelled. So what? So stinkin' what? Most of the people who mock you are lost anyway, and if you ask me, love is keeping your kid out of the street. Love is rescuing a person from a burning building. Love is sending people to the cross, and we can't do that unless we preserve God's word. If you are a Christian, you can't dismiss the Bible because you "feel" a certain way. I know it's tempting. It's definitely the easy way out. And while the Bible can feel offensive at times, that doesn't mean that it isn't Truth. The truth is, love does not mean "anything goes." God hates divorce. Biblical marriage is between a man and a woman. Abortion is taking a life. If I'm making you mad right now, take that up with God. He authored the Bible, not me. Loving you means leading you to Truth, not watering it down or dismissing it as archaic. Sister, I say these things because I care about your soul. I care about your peace. And most of all, I care about God's opinion more than yours. Does this give me the right to be a pompous Pharisee? Absolutely not, but I would not be loving you well if I tried to water down the words of God. And I love you. I'm for you. I pray that people love me and are for me, too.

While the Bible can feel offensive at times, that doesn't mean that it isn't Truth. The truth is, love does not mean "anything goes."

Quit hiding in church and pulling the "love" card. Quit sitting quietly while a fellow soccer mom spills about her affair. Quit being Switzerland when a girl in your Bible study laments over the Supreme Court's abortion decision. Ask her to coffee. To dinner. Give her a chance to speak. To be heard. Then do the hard thing and lead her to Truth. Not on social media. Not in an email. Face to face. Christian, you have to speak God's truth, politically, personally, always, because God's Truth is set. You know it, and I know it. Oh, if we could all have hearts like that of the prophet Jeremiah as he warned his people that their own actions would be their destruction.

> *My heart, my heart—I writhe in pain! My heart pounds within me! I can't be still.*
>
> Jeremiah 4:19 (NLT)

When is the last time you writhed in pain over abortion? When is the time you couldn't be still over this pronoun garbage? Because here's the deal. Fiery prophets like Jeremiah preach with broken hearts. They are broken over the sins of others, over the effect it has on the world. They are so broken that they can't be silent. Sister, this should be you. This should me. Get filled at church and go forth and speak up! Let's be prophets in this broken, sad, depraved world in which we live. Let's tell people, and show them by our lives, that a life in Jesus can be "radically different." When the disciples started their ministry with Jesus, Mark 6 describes the atmosphere:

> *Then they were on the road. They preached with joyful urgency that life can be radically different; right and left they sent the demons packing; they brought wellness to the sick, anointing their bodies, healing their spirits.*
>
> Mark 6:12–13 (MSG)

Joyful urgency? When was the last time you felt an urgency to share the gospel? We have to quit hiding behind our Bibles and tell our coworker she doesn't have to keep hooking up with people on Tinder. We have to say no to the third Bible study we are asked to be a part of and instead ask our unsaved neighbor to have dinner in our home. Their kids should be playing with our kids. What are we afraid of? Atheism is not contagious, but our joy for Jesus—that is *extremely* contagious. The disciples healed the broken. They brought healing for *emotional* pain. And before you argue and say, "Well, those were the *disciples*," let me remind you that the disciples were not the brightest, most godly folks. They were uneducated sinners. They were poor. They were normal guys. But they were willing. Be willing, sister. I know it's hard. I know it's scary. But we have to be willing.

So, what does sharing the gospel mean exactly? That can be a pretty intimidating ask, I know. Listen. I'm sure there are scenarios where people have their Bibles on tap and they're locked and loaded, ready when someone asks a "Jesus" question. They literally have a Scripture for every possible scenario. That's never happened to me. In fact, I've been known to panic and forget Scripture altogether when asked on the fly. So, if you are an inarticulate, regular Joe Blow like me, do yourself a favor. Don't try to perform. Don't over-spiritualize. And please don't rehearse. Just take people to your Jesus. Do your best to answer their questions. Seek answers when you don't know how to respond. But, more importantly, share what Jesus has done for you. People can argue theology all day long, but no one can tell you who Jesus is to you.

There's absolutely a time and place for discipleship and reading the Bible, but pretty much every time I share the gospel, it begins with my asking someone to tell me their story. Nine out of ten times, sharing the gospel consists of conversations had in the office or talking to other moms on the playground or soccer field. Recently, I asked my coworker why she didn't go to church anymore. She was brought up in it, listens to Christian music, yet she hasn't been inside a church since college. She told me that she believes church is filled with hypocritical elitists who don't give a (insert four-letter word) about the poor. I didn't see that coming, but I was thankful for her honesty. Now that I know her story, I know how to talk her. I know that she needs to see Jesus as someone who loves the poor, as a perfect man who despised the hypocrites of his day—an advocate for the underserved. At that point, she was not open to being asked to church. Sharing the gospel with her started by trying to show her that I practice what I preach—imperfectly, yes, but I wanted her to see me genuinely and authentically be the hands and feet of Jesus.

But make no mistake. While showing action is important, at a certain point I have to put on my big girl panties and have uncomfortable conversations with her. And before I can ask her to church, given what she's told me about her past, I feel like I should simply be her friend. With joyful urgency, we go to lunch. We text. That's how it begins. Don't think for one second you have to be more prepared than that.

Just ask Rosaria Butterfield. Her story of meeting Jesus is radical. She was a gay, feminist professor from Upstate New York. She was basically the kind of person I would write off as a lost cause. I hate to say that, but before reading her story, I would have never approached someone with her background. Her PhD alone would have intimidated me into silence. That and the fact that she was an expert in women's studies and had a live-in girlfriend. I would have assumed that her mind was made up. Well, someone did talk to her. A pastor. Only he didn't try to "un-gay" her or even ask her to church. He started having meals with her after she wrote an argumentative letter to him about his ministry. His response moved her. Over time, they formed a friendship. He and his wife gathered together with her in their home and in hers. Y'all! He just joined her world and trusted Jesus to do the rest—and he did. Rosaria is now a believer and has written many books. She's reached so many people all because this man was obedient.

I have to ask myself, "How many people have I passed by because I assumed they would not be open to the gospel?" Sister, how many people have you passed by? Because here's the truth. People who don't know Jesus are going to hell. I don't say that to be mean. On the contrary, I say it with the heaviest of hearts. I say it because we all know unbelievers. You're probably thinking of one right now, and it's probably someone you love. Hear me when I say this. There is nothing more important than sharing the gospel with whoever needs to hear it. Stop waiting for your coworker to ask—she won't. Stop waiting for your brother-in-law to ask—he won't. It's our responsibility to tell them. Quit hiding *behind* your Bible and *live* the Bible. Quit hiding at church by spending all your time there and *be* the church. There is nothing more important on this planet than making sure people come to know Christ as their Lord and Savior.

As I approach the midlife mark, I have a burning desire to point people to Jesus. I'm done hiding him away in my heart as if he is *my* secret, *my* powerful ring. If this means I need to drink a margarita at happy hour with someone, then I will. If this means I need to refrain from wine, then I will. If this means I need to change my friend group, then I will. If this means I need a new job, then I'll get one, because, pointing people to Jesus should take precedence over losing weight, eating more greens, or paying off debt. This is why we were created. It scares me that we Jesus followers aren't burning to share him with others. We will literally flood our social media with restaurant recommendations, workout tips, and recipes. But share Jesus with someone who needs him? Nope.

The great Charles Spurgeon says it better than anyone I know:

If sinners will be damned, at least let them leap to hell over our bodies. And if they will perish, let them perish with our arms about their knees, imploring them to stay. If hell must be filled, at least let it be filled in the teeth of our exertions, and let no one go there unwarned and unprayed for.[3]

I don't know about you, but I want to be found clinging to the knees of my neighbors and family. I want to be intentional. I want my conversations to have meaning. Do you know why? Because Jesus chose me. And guess what else? Jesus chose you. I know it's awkward. I know you feel uncomfortable, but guess what? This isn't all on you. God is doing so much behind-the-scenes prep work that we know nothing of. My coworker I told you about who was burned at church? The one who hates hypocrites? Well, she's starting to ask questions. She's starting to tell me more and more of her story. She even asked me for a devotional book. And while I have no idea what will happen, I can tell you this: I will be found clinging to her knees. Y'all, God does not need you to be awesome. He doesn't need you to have the Bible memorized. He doesn't need you running every committee at church. He needs you to be willing. He needs you to let *him* be awesome. And the work he will do through an obedient child is astounding.

And then he told them, "Go into all the world and preach the Good News to everyone."

Mark 16:15 (NLT)

---

[3]Tom Carter, comp., *Spurgeon at His Best: Over 2000 Striking Quotations from the World's Most Exhaustive and Widely-Read Sermon Series* (Grand Rapids, MI: Baker Book House, 1988), 67.

18

Sisters, for the love.

*Do you know that nothing you do in this
life will ever matter, unless it is about
loving God and loving the people he made?*

*Francis Chan, Crazy Love: Overwhelmed
by a Relentless God*

THROUGHOUT THE GOSPELS, Jesus rebuked one particular group of people over and over again. It wasn't promiscuous women. It wasn't gays, whores, drunks, or lawbreakers. Nope. It wasn't even the man who betrayed him. It was actually the super-religious known as the Pharisees—the know-it-all scholars who knew the law so well they often recited it but never lived it. They bullied the very people Christ actually came to Earth to serve. In this modern day, I equate the Pharisees to be arrogant Christians who talk a lot. You know who I'm talking about. You may even have a few in mind. These are the people who sit on church committees and have lots of opinions about sinners yet rarely live out the gospel. They are the ones who believe homosexuals shouldn't be allowed in church—so as not to condone their sin, of course. That Muslims should be hated—after all, they all wear bombs under their shirts. They think the homeless man under the bridge needs to get a job.

Pharisees are full of hot, dangerous air. They are religious bullies who never seem to get their hands dirty. They love to talk about how holy they are. They pray using big, intimidating words, but here's the kicker: they miss the point. Completely. They repel the unchurched with their intimidation and judgment. They leave Christians wounded. They push the lost closer toward hell. Take Muslims, for example. I get that some people in their religion are radical. I also understand that, because of 9/11 and other horrific events carried out by Muslim extremists, many have generalized this entire group and have become fearful. But does that make it right? Does that make it true? Does that mean we're to look away when we see a Muslim lady at Target? Is she not a human being who needs to know about that radical love of a reckless God? Is she beyond saving? Am I so smart that I think I know God's story for her?

What about the growing community of people who self-identify with non-heterosexual terms? Are you repelled by this group? Are you afraid they will convert your children if you invite them into your home? Here's a thought. How about you introduce them to Jesus and let him work that out in their hearts and in ours. I was once told by a well-respected and trusted leader in ministry that he doesn't believe that he should break bread with homosexuals in his home. *Are you kidding me?* I think he may have slept through seminary when they studied the life of Jesus. But to be fair, we all say things like this because we're uncomfortable. Y'all, we have to get over ourselves, because here's the deal. When Jesus told us to love one another. When he modeled love so perfectly, he didn't mean to love only the lovable. That's easy. Anyone can do that. But Jesus loved those who were seen as outcasts. He loved the dirty, messy people who are actually quite difficult to love. He loved the super sinful. He *loves* the super sinful.

Truth is, we're uncomfortable with sins different than what we've become accustomed to. Mainstream sins like gluttony, drinking, and gossip, those seem to be acceptable, yet bringing a stripper or a drug addict to church—no way. Off-limits. Don't bring them to our beautiful church. Their presence will scare people. Okay, this deserves an eye roll. Or perhaps a slap in the face. Christians should ache to share the radical love that Jesus shows us daily. We should want nothing more than to love God and to love people. Because if you truly think someone is going to hell, shouldn't that make you want to take them to church and break bread with them in your home?

Let me ask you a question. How often do you have the urgency to share the gospel? I want you to set this book down and really think about what I'm asking. How often do you lavish love on your neighbor in attempts to show them your God? How often does the thought of your loved one going to hell terrify you into action? Y'all, we can't show up to church Sunday after Sunday, raise our hands in worship, sit on our little church committee, and move on. That's not enough. Not enough by a long shot. You and I are commanded to spread the gospel. The good news. And while the "who" and "how" looks different for everyone, it's a must. It's actually our highest calling.

But I'm no saint. Or evangelist. Or missionary. It can be a struggle for me as well. I know it's awkward to talk about Jesus sometimes, especially to someone with no church background. I wish I had a step-by-step guide on what you should say or do, but to be honest, no such plan exists. In fact, I recently screwed up when trying to share Jesus with a neighbor. Now, this guy is smart. I mean, engineer-minded, "reads philosophy" kind of smart. To say he annihilated me with knowledge is an understatement. I babbled like an idiot as he refuted everything I said with facts and quoted other texts than the Bible. The more he talked, the more awkward I became.

In hindsight, I wish I had just listened. I wish I had just asked him questions about his story and how he got to where he was. I wish I had asked him why he is so angry. I wish I had asked him why I'm so annoying to him. I wish I had asked him who he puts his trust in when he's afraid. I wish I had asked him who he thanks when he sees a beautiful sunset. I wish I had done so many things that I didn't do. But I messed up. I tried to be in control and answer everything he threw my way. Y'all, you will never be able to give all the answers. No one has all the answers. And guess what? You shouldn't even try to have them. Truth is, no one comes to Jesus through debating. No one comes to Jesus because you one-upped them or finally answered some crazy question of theirs. Nope. People come to Jesus through love. And I was so concerned with defending myself that I didn't show this man what he needed most from me: love. But guess what? It ain't over. I still have breath in my lungs and this man still talks to me. So I'm going to stay at it. I'm going to stay at this neighbor. I'm going to pray for him. I'm going to befriend his wife. I'm gonna show this family Jesus if it kills me. I can take them meals. I can have my kids play with their kids. I can pray for more opportunities—but guess what? Even if this man moves away tomorrow, even if I screw up again, God can reach this man. Truth is, God can save this man by any means he wishes. He doesn't need my help to do it. But he has placed me in this person's path, and for that reason, obedience is required.

I recently watched a video by well-known magician and self-proclaimed atheist Penn Jillette that was life-changing. He was approached after a show by a Christian who quite gently shared the gospel with him. While Jillette still proclaims there is no God, he was grateful. Here's what he said:

> *I've always said that I don't respect people who don't proselytize. I don't respect that at all. If you believe that there's a heaven and hell, and people could be going to hell or not getting eternal life, or whatever, and you think that it's not really worth telling them this because it would make it socially awkward—and atheists who think people shouldn't proselytize, just leave me alone, keep your religion to yourself—how much do you have to hate somebody to not proselytize? How much do you have to hate somebody to believe that everlasting life is possible and not tell them that? I mean, if I believed, beyond the shadow of a doubt, that a truck was coming at you, and you didn't believe that truck was bearing down on you, there is a certain point where I tackle you. And this is more important than that.[4]*

We are so quick to recommend a lipstick color to our mom friends. We share recipes, give parental advice and dinner recommendations. But sharing the gospel to someone headed to hell? Nope. Never. That is not PC.

The more I read Scripture, the more it becomes clear that everything we do really comes down to two things: loving God and loving people. You see, if you love God you will strive to be like Jesus. In fact, this over-flow of love for the Lord is what actually drives our behavior. This love for Jesus is also what drives us to love others. It's not the law. It's not the Ten Commandments. Sure, obedience is great and God wants our obedi-ence, but love is what causes us to want to be obedient. The Pharisees got

---

[4]beinzee, "A Gift of a Bible," YouTube, July 8, 2010, https://tinyurl.com/Jilletteclip.

it wrong. They obeyed the law but lacked love. And if we aren't careful, we may do the same.

> *But when the Pharisees heard that he had silenced the Sadducees with his reply, they met together to question him again. One of them, an expert in religious law, tried to trap him with this question: "Teacher, which is the most important commandment in the law of Moses?"*
>
> *Jesus replied, "'You must love the Lord your God with all your heart, all your soul, and all your mind.' This is the first and greatest commandment. A second is equally important: 'Love your neighbor as yourself.' The entire law and all the demands of the prophets are based on these two commandments."*
>
> Matthew 22:34–40 (NLT)

Let's be honest. Loving Jesus isn't hard. Sure, there are times where we struggle with understanding his goodness, but come on. How hard is it to love the creator of the universe, the one who sent his son to die in our place? But loving people, that's a whole other beast. In 1 John 4, John refers back to Jesus' top two commands:

> *We love each other because he loved us first. If someone says, "I love God," but hates a fellow believer, that person is a liar; for if we don't love people we can see, how can we love God, whom we cannot see? And he has given us this command: Those who love God must also love their fellow believers.*
>
> 1 John 4:19-21 (NLT)

I hate to burst bubbles here, but John isn't referring to your blood relatives when he says "brother" here (though that can be hard at times). What this verse is saying is that if you love God, you will love *all* people. This means loving people who treat you poorly. Those who use you. Basically, anyone who makes you uncomfortable. I'm not saying we are to ignore sin. I'm also not saying we should be doormats with no boundaries. What I am saying, however, is that it's God's job to judge. You aren't Judge Judy. He doesn't need you to hammer down the gavel. What you can do, however, what we should do, is love people in such a radical way that they can't help but want to know our Jesus. You aren't condoning their sin. You're simply pointing them to the one who died for those sins. And there's no conviction if there's no Jesus. So, do yourself a favor and throw all that negative energy toward loving God and toward loving people. Easier said than done, I know. But after a while you realize you don't have to carry the burden of the how and when. The Holy Spirit does all the heavy lifting. You simply show love.

> **You and I are commanded to spread the gospel. The good news. And while the "who" and "how" looks different for everyone, it's a must. It's actually our highest calling.**

A few months ago I took a look at my life and I realized that most, if not all of my friends looked like me, talked like me, and believed like me. Most of them had the same socioeconomic status and basically the same upbringing as me. The more I immersed myself into new parts of my city, the more it became clear that this is not the way the church is meant to look. I'm not saying you have to stop going to your home church because it's predominantly one race or that you need to get all new friends or move. What I am saying is God wants us to love all people. Christian and non-Christian. Rich and poor. Liberal and conservative. And they crazy thing is that the differences that divide us are nothing new. Sure the dividing line changes, but actual division has always been an issue. In Colossians 3:11 Paul pointed this out to the church in Colossae:

> *In this new life, it doesn't matter if you are a Jew or a Gentile, circumcised or uncircumcised, barbaric, uncivilized, slave, or free. Christ is all that matters, and he lives in all of us.*
>
> Colossians 3:11 (NLT)

I will be the first to admit I've struggled with this. Actually, I've wrestled with it a great deal because this makes me very uncomfortable. Out of my own insecurity, I've convinced myself that I shouldn't go to certain places or be with certain people. And in some instances, I shouldn't. But in most cases I was also living in a delusional bubble. I was so worried about what someone might think if they saw me at a bar or restaurant having a drink or found out I had atheist friends or gay friends. Seriously, the other day I ran into the liquor store to buy a bottle of wine on the way to dinner club and found myself telling the checkout guy that I was only going to have a glass. Or two, I added. But only if I ate a lot. Two and through, I said about ten times. I went on to tell him my entire church background. This was ridiculous. I am ridiculous. If letting down your guard and intentionally widening your circle of influence seems over-whelming to you, like it does me, read the Gospels. Pick one: Matthew, Mark, Luke, or John. Read it again and again. Read about all the places Jesus went. This will give you the grace to go into those places as well. But make no mistake. While Jesus went to the places where he could find sinners, he was most definitely in Christian community. His mission was anchored in God. And he never sinned.

Widen your circle, yes, but don't go it alone. Jesus had the Twelve, whom he loved deeply. These were the men he prayed with, ate with, and basically did life with. And when he was gone, they had each other. I can't say this next part with enough urgency. All of us should have a tribe. The ones who call us out on our sin. Who pray with us and lament with us. Those we can be vulnerable with. I don't care if you are an introvert or struggle with friendships—this is nonnegotiable. You are a fool not to have accountability. These are the people who anchor you so you can go to the hard places. These are the people who point out your blind spots. These are the people who point you to Jesus. Who are your twelve?

Jesus also spent precious alone time with the Father. If you aren't spending time like that with Jesus, you need to change that. Yesterday. But what is intriguing to me is that he also ate with tax collectors and spoke about intimate subjects with women who were considered shame-ful. This was progressive. He hung out with the social outcasts—and we should too. He also healed the no-names. The ugly. The helpless. The pathetic. Those who had nothing to offer him in return. Jesus went out of his way to love those *not* in church. He didn't have brunch with the church leaders at the country club. He went to find the sinners and the shamed. But don't miss the fact that while he went to those places, he never once joined them in their sin. Jesus never changed his character, regardless of where he was. He didn't find the need to tweak his message to make it more relatable. Basking in cultural norms for the sake of not scaring off new believers is unnecessary. Jesus was strategic and purposeful in all his encounters—but uncompromising. We should be too.

As a mother, I want nothing more than for my children to love Jesus. In my need to shelter and "protect" them, I have done them a great disservice by turning my back on the people Christ has put in my path. If I were to continue, I would be raising a bunch of Pharisees. As they grow older and start their own families, I want them to remember their mom as someone who loved sinners. I want their "normal" to be breaking bread with people of every race, religion, and socioeconomic status. Does this mean I let my children sit at a table while someone curses profusely or gets wasted? Absolutely not. Does this mean I take shots with my coworker? No way. But it does mean I invite the lost into my home to serve them at my table. To invite them to fellowship with those I love most, my children, regardless of our differences. Sister, we have to invite the lost to our table. We have to love them. We have to get our fill from the Lord, from our twelve, and go forth into the hard places. The gospel was never meant to be held in secret. We have to share the good news one person at a time.

But God showed his great love for us by sending Christ to die for us while we were still sinners.

Romans 5:8 (NLT)

19

Sister, know his game.

*Did God really say, "You must not eat
from any tree in the garden"?*
Satan (Genesis 3:1)

I ALWAYS IMAGINED SATAN to be a skinny little man in a red body suit. With a pitchfork, of course. As I got older, my view of him changed. I pictured him as something really scary. Like in the movies when a bunch of kids get hold of a Ouija board. As I reach the middle-age mark in life, I realize how off I've been on both extremes. While Satan and hell are scary and absolutely real, I'm of the opinion that a lot of us have missed the mark in understanding who Satan is and what he's capable of. Sadly, in that faulty thinking, we have become easy targets. Let me ask you: If your car broke down on the side of the road at night, would you get in a truck with a shady driver who has creepy eyes and a scary-looking face? Would you get in a Beamer on a warm, sunny day with someone who looks like Bradley Cooper?

The things of Satan are attractive. I mean, Bradley Cooper, fancy-car attractive. That's the scary part. That's what makes you an easy target. He draws you in. He's not some red-suit-wearing freak. He's a sneaky salesperson who comes at you with everything you've ever wanted in this life. Second Corinthians 11:14 says that he disguises himself as an angel of light. And the scariest thing about Satan is that he's patient. He's observant. He's an expert on you. In fact, he has a tailor-made plan for your unraveling.

Like a custom pair of designer jeans, Satan's plan for you is a perfect fit and looks good on you. His tactics are personal. He's strategic. And he hates you. He hates your guts. His mission is to destroy you. He's also smart. He knows his fate. He knows God will ultimately end his game and the worst kind of being has nothing to lose. This means that he is all in. He wants your family. He wants your kids. He absolutely wants your marriage. And there is no way he is going to let you use your gifts. He wants you racist. He wants your heart hardened to the poor. He wants you living in mediocrity. He wants you to hate the way you look. He wants your peace. He wants your contentment. He wants you to numb your pain with alcohol and Netflix and busyness. He wants you self-focused. He wants you jealous of other people. He wants you to be bored with the Bible. He wants you to struggle with your weight. He wants you just satisfied enough to not need God. He wants you to question God's goodness.

> **Like a custom pair of designer jeans, Satan's plan for you is a perfect fit and looks good on you. His tactics are personal. He's strategic. And he hates you.**

Y'all, Satan wants to destroy you. Forgive the blatant intensity, but there's no way to sugarcoat it. There is a real force out to get you, and it's not through witchcraft and exorcisms like you see in the movies. I can't end this book without urging you to watch your back. It's my duty as your sister in Christ to warn you. To beg you to call this loser out. To empower you. To help you recognize his schemes. Most of all, I want to remind you that Satan will be defeated. One day God will whip his sorry tail and he will get his. Scripture promises us that, but until then, keep your eyes open. Satan can't have your soul, but, my stars, he can steal your joy, and he can sideline you from God's work. In fact, that's his primary goal. He wants to take you out of the game completely. Don't you dare let him.

Pay attention! I beg you to recognize his game and refute it. I plead with you to fight for joy. To stay in the game. To speak the Scriptures out loud. To confess your sins. To repent from them. To be in community. I don't care if it's with one person or a dozen—let someone in, because being alone without anyone to watch your back and call you out is the scariest place to be. In fact, Satan wants you to hide the deepest parts of yourself so he can tell you *his* version of you. He wants you to wish you married someone else. He wants you to turn on the TV and turn off your real life. He wants you to be so insecure that you won't leave the house. He wants you to hate being a mother. He wants you to flirt with your coworker. He wants you to helicopter your kids. He wants you to emotionally eat. He wants you numb to conviction. That's why he comes at you with everything you think you want. Comfort—that's his biggest MO. Don't be naive to this. First Peter 5:8 says:

> *Keep a cool head. Stay alert. The Devil is poised to pounce, and would like nothing better than to catch you napping. Keep your guard up.*
>
> 1 Peter 5:8 (MSG)

No one gets to fly under his radar. He is coming after all of us. So, what's a girl to do? I'm glad you asked. Play or be played, sister.

The enemy trembles when your knees hit the floor to pray. So, pray. Pray like your life depends on it. Pray for your children. Pray for your marriage. Pray for this country. Pray for your enemies. Pray for your brothers and sisters. Pray for yourself. Because if you're kicking butt for the kingdom, if you're sharing the gospel, if you're using your gifts, he will be on your tail—not as an eerie force, but as a distraction. Recognize this and fight this sorry loser back. I know it's hard. The days can be so long. Monotony can suck you dry. There are days when marriage can seem like a prison sentence and parenting can suck. Loving an imperfect community can wear you out. Being vulnerable can be next to impossible. But don't stop. That's what Satan wants. Keep relating to others. Keep showing up. Keep praying. Keep confessing. And remember, God wins. No matter what this life throws at you, you are on a winning team.

It has been a great privilege to write these words to you. It has breathed life into my own soul. I love you for that. I may not know you, but I can still love you. I love you for letting me be honest about my messy life. I love you for reading my words so that I can be held accountable to what I'm writing. I love you for being different. I love you for your perspective. I love you for your gifts. But guess what? My love pales in comparison to the Lord's love for you. Your husband, your kids, your childhood bestie, your children, your mother—not one of these human beings is capable of loving you like the one who died for you. There's someone so much greater who knows you intimately. Someone who sees into your soul. Someone who claims you. Someone who designed you. Someone who has great things in store for you. Sister, as long as you have breath in your lungs, you have purpose. And nothing—I mean *nothing* can scare away the love of Jesus. No sin. No thought process. No mistake. Nothing. So live wild and free anchored in the one who died for you. Godspeed.

> *And I am convinced that nothing can ever separate us from God's love. Neither death nor life, neither angels nor demons, neither our fears for today nor our worries about tomorrow—not even the powers of hell can separate us from God's love. No power in the sky above or in the earth below—indeed, nothing in all creation will ever be able to separate us from the love of God that is revealed in Christ Jesus our Lord.*
>
> Romans 8:38–39 (NLT)

Meet Kim

KIM DAFFERNER IS a voice to be reckoned with, speaking truth to women of faith in a raw, vulnerable, witty, conversational style that both charms and alarms the reader, plunging us through the mess of her choices and experiences to get to the message of Jesus, the cost of sin, and the power of redemption.

Kim has a lot of identities—a wife of Andrew since 2009; a mom of four, which includes a son waiting for her in heaven; a social worker; a writer; a woman full of the same insecurities, faults, and wounds we all relate to—but she would prefer to be known just as a girl who loves Jesus.

Sister, I Feel Ya is Kim's first nonfiction book, a challenging deep inner dive into the ways women hurt each other, themselves, and the people they love the most, an honest view of the ways women process pain, and a call to women of faith to wake up and face their own personal compromises, return to holiness, and find themselves again in the arms of Jesus.

Kim's first book, *Tall Skinny Cappuccino*, a charming, light, and clean rom-com, was published in 2008, and may see a reboot and sequel in its future.

To connect with Kim, inquire about speaking or interviews:

Email: kdafferner@gmail.com

Or through the publisher: info@encouragebooks.com

Bulk pricing available to resellers and non-profits through Ingram or through the publisher: (812)987-6148 or info@encouragebooks.com